Costume Jewelers
The Golden Age of Design

Dedication

This book is lovingly dedicated to my husband, Robert Ball, without whose encouragement and labors my "adventure in jewelry" never would have come to fruition; and to the memory of my parents, Tora Carlson Dubbs and John F. Dubbs, an artist who was involved in the design and manufacture of jewelry for much of his adult life. I hope my efforts will, in some measure, fulfill his dreams.

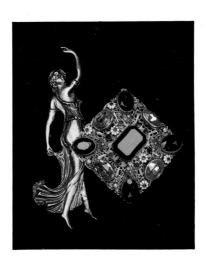

Costume Jewelers

The Golden Age of Design

Revised & Expanded 3rd Edition

Joanne Dubbs Ball

Schiffer Publishing Ltd

4880 Lower Valley Road, Atglen, PA 19310 USA

Acknowledgments

Paul Steinman at Accessocraft; Lisa Paglia at Anne Klein; Abigail Apisdorf and Michael Laux; Sandra Boucher; Josette Donetto and Diane Delaney at Cardin; Laura Miller at Cartier; Jackie Rogers at Ciner; Laura Bartels; Lawrence Kasoff; Karl Eisenberg; Ray Feig; Arthur Freirich and Ann Winship; Alfred Gaita at Pell; Robert and James Hobé; Joan Castle Joseff; Alan Kramer; Kenneth Jay Lane and staff; Bernard Shapiro and Yvette Brownstein at Les Bernard; Beth Miller and Pat Boyle at Napier; Diane McLoone at Monet; Amadeo Panetta; Pamela and Christina Polcini; Anne Magnin for Adele Simpson; Lester and Sol Smith; Trisha Lee and Rachelle Neuman at Trifari; Paul Verrecchia; Lou Valente at Swank; Ellen and John Wagman; Christine de St. Andreieu at Yves Saint Laurent.

Kudos to Conrad Vout, who helped me get started in my jewelry collecting "spree," and Kris Blauvelt, who urged me to "go for it" in the first place! Also to Sid Schatsky and Shelley Geffner for their special assistance and who, along with Francoise Landrum, Mary Anne Johnstone, Mary McMahon, Robin Sandler and Alla Jacobson afforded me the opportunity to add many outstanding pieces to my collection. Thanks also to Joellen Hopkins, to my neighbors, Lou Acker and Herb Young, for their computer expertise, and to Bertha Young for being my patient reader.

Very special thanks to Dorothy and Milton Torem for sharing their knowledge of the jewelry business with me, with gratitude beyond measure to Dorothy for her time, effort and expertise in photographing her Chanel and Givenchy collections as well as her wonderful Schiaparelli hatbox - and for giving me access to her vast collection of *Harper's Bazaar* magazines. All have added immeasurably to the ambiance of this book, and I will be forever grateful! To all the good folks at Schiffer Publishing, especially Tim Scott for his photographic expertise - and delightful sense of humor - my deep appreciation. And thanks beyond measure to Nancy and Peter Schiffer, who liked my idea and gave me their unequivocable support in pursuing it. Words cannot fully express my gratitude for their encouragement, confidence and friendship.

Revised price guide: 2000
Copyright © 1990, 1997 & 2000 by Joanne Dubbs Ball.
Library of Congress Catalog Card Number: 99-69614

ISBN: 0-7643-1084-4
Printed in China
1 2 3 4

Published by Schiffer Publishing Ltd.
4880 Lower Valley Road
Atglen, PA 19310
Phone: (610) 593-1777; Fax: (610) 593-2002
E-mail: Schifferbk@aol.com
Please visit our web site catalog at **www.schifferbooks.com**

In Europe, Schiffer books are distributed by Bushwood Books
6 Marksbury Avenue Kew Gardens
Surrey TW9 4JF England
Phone: 44 (0)208-392-8585; Fax: 44 (0)208-392-9876
E-mail: Bushwd@aol.com
Free postage in the UK., Europe; air mail at cost.

This book may be purchased from the publisher.
Include $3.95 for shipping. Please try your bookstore first.
We are always looking for authors to write books on new and related subjects.
If you have an idea for a book please contact us at the address above.
You may write for a free printed catalog.

Contents

Foreword

As a collector and dealer specializing in vintage designer jewelry, I've especially enjoyed my personal contact with folks who are eager for details about the golden age of costume jewelry design (concentrating mainly on the period of the 1930s through the 1970s), and especially for more definitive information on the individual designers who made this such an exciting time. Hopefully, this book will answer many of those questions, pique the interest of the novice, and be a useful reference tool for the seasoned collector.

Realistically, few of us can afford to purchase the "real thing," except in small pieces like simple gold chains and earrings, or a few gold rings with precious or semi-precious gems. Although much of the costume jewelry from this period was deliberately designed to look "fabulously fake" (that's part of the fun of owning and wearing it), others are barely discernible from treasured pieces now securely resting in vaults and safety deposit boxes.

Thus, we have the best of both worlds at our fingertips. Depending on our mood and the outfit we wish to complement, we can, on the one hand, be elegantly regal and, on the other, boldly outrageous. And, when we're feeling especially adventuresome, we can enjoy the challenge of experimenting - large, showy pieces on a cashmere sweater or jacket, rhinestones and opulent earrings with denims, brooches fastened to an upturned hat brim, a trio of unusual bracelets climbing the arm of a simple dress. All reflect what most designers had in mind...a sense of beauty combined with an air of playfulness!

Following are brief biographies and illustrations of the designs of many of the most-respected names from that era. With literally hundreds of companies and designers producing jewelry in what was then a burgeoning industry, it would be virtually impossible to elaborate on the backgrounds of all of them, or to feature examples of each artisan's work, even if such were available. Additionally, many individuals from the past are unfortunately no longer with us, and information is available only through the recollections of those people who continue to work in the industry or have retired but can still be contacted.

The jewelry business was, and still is, a large and complex network of designers, manufacturers and sales representatives. Without the cooperation of many of these individuals who still remember "the good old days," this book could never have been completed.

With apologies to those whose names are not included and those about whom I could acquire only limited background, please know that the following is a tribute to them all!

I would be remiss if I neglected to point out that although terms like "quality of workmanship" and "innovative" must, of necessity, be used time and again on the following pages (and I acknowledge in advance what may seem to be redundancy), it's nevertheless astonishing how varied the individual jewelry lines are - one bearing little resemblance to another. Viewed from a somewhat different perspective, this experience could be compared to reviews of a Broadway play. Many theater experiences over the past 50 years were described as "innovative," "thought provoking," and "spellbinding." Yet each play was unique - one totally different from the other in content and presentation. And so it is with the art form of jewelry making. Contrary to the popular maxim, there is indeed always *something* new under the sun!

While researching material for this book, it has been particularly heart-warming to discover that many of these businesses were, and still are, family operated. Sons and daughters have followed their parents and grandparents into a profession that has obviously been the source of much loyalty and affection. As Paul Verrecchia, founder of Lianna Inc. and son of renowned artist and jewelry designer Alfeo Verrecchia, mentioned in our telephone conversation, "Although it may at times be a real grind, this is essentially a *happy* business." I can only add - it shows!

Finally, if I were asked to give just one bit of advice to jewelry enthusiasts, it would be to wear and enjoy the pieces you own. They will serve you well.

Preface to the Third Edition

As noted in my preface to the Second Edition, unauthorized reproductions and fraudulent pieces bearing the markings of many giants from costume jewelry's "golden age" were then flooding the market. Sadly, the practice has escalated even further. How unfortunate that the general public, collectors, and even dealers, have been conned into paying high prices for fraudulent items that were purchased in good faith. Because of this uncertainty as to what's authentic and what isn't, sales by legitimate dealers have suffered, as have the values of long-standing collections. What-ever the case, buyers armed with the facts can still fight back!

As might be expected, it is the well-respected and high-end names that are the most vulnerable. Chief among these are Eisenberg, Hobe, Trifari, Coro, CoroCraft, and Boucher, but the practice is now so widespread that buyers should be careful with all their purchases. Be especially cautious with figurals, which are particularly popular today. Chief among these are *purported* jelly bellies, usually with glass bellies instead of the original acrylic. Some pieces display logos of companies that never made these or similar designs, as is the case with fraudulent jelly bellies marked Boucher. Certain pieces are from pirated copies of earlier designs, while others are "bastardized" offerings that were never part of the company's repertoire. Although some are skillful in their execution, most can be spotted by their inferior quality, gaudy stones, and glued on or incorrect logos. Sometimes manufactured in Asia, many of these fakes have the appearance one associates with other low-end imports from this area. Another widespread practice is to set all new stones directly into the bases of old pieces--pieces that were either broken, in such bad shape as to render them worthless to the market, or missing most or all of their original stones. Others have been crafted from molds that imitate the real thing. Thus, the unsuspecting buyer sees the old backing with its logo intact and pays hard-earned money for a piece that isn't authentic and has literally been rebuilt. (On the other hand, a small stone here or there can occasionally be replaced in otherwise perfect vintage pieces with no loss to its value, if professionally done.)

My advice is to seek out dealers who are knowledgable and familar with their sources...and don't hesitate to ask questions. It's upsetting to have a shopper proudly display a brooch pur-ported to be the work of their favorite company, and then be crestfallen when they discover the piece is not authentic. Whether costing $25 or several hundred, the buyer has squandered money...and their trust has been compromised. Sadly, we should be ever mindful of the dedicated artisans, some of whom are no longer with us, whose names have been besmirched in the process. Nevertheless, although profit has been gained under false pretenses, I remain hopeful that this too shall pass, and that these disquieting setbacks will never succeed in quelling our appreciation of the past...and the treasures it brought us!

Joanne Dubbs Ball
March, 2000

The World of Fashion and Jewelry Design

One thing the jewelry designer has over most designers is that his product can be worn any-where. Shoes have to stay with the feet. Hats are worn on the head. But jewelry can perch from hats all the way down the figure to the tip of the shoes. We're not restricted by materials. Nor by color. Nor by the problem of sizes as in some other accessories.

Irving Apisdorf
Vice President, Hattie Carnegie
Jewelry Division
(lecturing at a fashion careers course in the early 1960s)

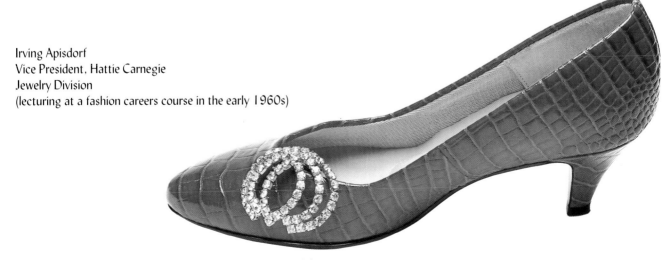

11

COLLECTION CAVIAR FROM PARIS

1. Chanel's Indian replica—a lace collar of imitation jewels to wear with a brushed-up coiffure

2. Her berry-cluster earrings—of red and green and pearl beads

3. Patou's delicate-tinted porcelain rose, nodding on a gold stem

4. Schiaparelli's coat-of-arms clip—a shield of gold metal, paved with bright simulated stones

5. Chanel's new coiffure-hat—a chou of velvet ribbons to set atop up-swept hair

6. Schiaparelli's flexible caterpillar, made of gold metal

7. Chanel's glove-jewels, red flowers for knuckles and wrist

8. Her gold metal cigarette-box with serpent-eye green stones

9. Schiaparelli's mermaid clip

10. Her playing-card clip of gold metal studded with bright stones

The designs were endless, the talent was enormous, and their contributions to the golden age of the costume jewelry industry were immeasurable, for although a dress is a dress is a dress, an outfit with complementary accessories (a stunning brooch, jeweled belt, dramatic necklace) is no longer "just a dress." Instead, it becomes an individual fashion statement that takes the garment one step beyond the designer's original vision.

How natural then that so many renowned fashion designers affixed their names to beautiful and imaginative costume jewelry. For they were just that - jewels to be added to the wearer's costume, whether it be a simple dress, coat, or suit, or the most elaborate formal gown.

The list of these designers, whose names appear on the backs and clasps of some of the most inspired pieces from this "golden age," reads like a "who's who" of the fashion industry: Carnegie, Rosenstein, Schiaparelli, Chanel - the list goes on and on. Just as each garment bears its individual mark of distinction, so, too, does each accessory.

The stylized pieces of many designers are easily recognized without searching for their signature. Indeed, the message conveyed in the settings and overall imagery makes them as distinctive as the fashions bearing their labels. From the whimsical quality of Hattie Carnegie's oriental groupings and animal pieces to the stylish, Deco beauty of Nettie Rosenstein's sterling brooches, each created an added dimension to the designer's repertoire.

In this fashion designer section, it's important to bear in mind that, like other accessories and related items, the manufacture of their jewelry was and in some cases still is a licensed operation. Nevertheless, the famous names for whom this jewelry was created never underestimated the inherent value of accessorizing and its importance to the garment, whether of their own design or "off the rack."

And, as you will see, many of them instigated the bold ideas behind their jewelry, frequently dealing directly with the designers and manufacturers in critical phases of the production.

The following is a salute to these giants from the world of couture. They contributed much to the appreciation and acceptance of costume jewelry as a vital adjunct to the complex world of fashion.

Any tribute would be incomplete, however, if we failed to recognize that vast network of talented designers and artisans who actually created this jewelry we admire today. Fortunately, many of them continue to make enormous contributions to the world of fashion jewelry. For that we are doubly grateful. Hats off to them all!

Left to right: Circular mother-of-pearl insets are surrounded by rhinestones in this Carnegie bracelet, $75-125; tiny red stones are interwoven with gold strands in these dainty, raised-heart earrings, $100-150; a dramatic rhinestone and crystal necklace with matching earrings will be magically transformed, depending on the fabric it rests against, $300-400.

Hattie Carnegie

Born in 1886 in Vienna, Austria, Hattie Carnegie came to the United States at the tender age of six. Born Hattie Kanengeiser, she later changed Kanengeiser to Carnegie because, for her, it typified the great American success story. Little did she know that this prophetic choice would lead to yet another Carnegie legacy of success, one that would be equally as amazing, especially when accomplished by a woman in what was still essentially "a man's world"!

Carnegie's father died when she was only 11 years old, and she was forced to leave school and go to work. She was briefly a messenger at Macy's, a pin girl in a millinery workroom, and an assistant in a dress house. All these experiences combined to give her the determination to succeed in some area of the fashion industry, and at the age of 23 she formed a partnership with her seamstress friend Rose Roth. Rose concentrated on sewing the garments while Hattie applied her talent to hats. Within a few years, Carnegie was sole owner of the business. Only four feet ten inches tall, her height was certainly not indicative of the giantlike stature she was destined to achieve in the competitive world of couture, for the Carnegie business acumen eventually built an $8 million fashion empire.

Each year, Carnegie established a pattern of evaluating the foreign fashion market by making numerous trips to Paris. She had an inherent sense of the taste of American women, skillfully converting the European mood into garments with an American flair. In so doing she established herself as a fashion maven for American couture buyers abroad, and was treated with equal respect by her French counterparts. In fact, during this period she left an especially unforgettable "signature" on the fashion world, which quickly became a generic term in the industry - the "little Carnegie suit."

There was another fashion venture, however, that brought her special honors - one quite different from those that had gone before or any that came after. In 1950 she used this basic "little Carnegie suit" and converted it to the new uniforms for the Women's Army Corps, the Army Nurse Corps, and the Women's Medical Specialist Corps, earning her the Army's highest civilian award.

Throughout her career, Carnegie became mentor to an impressive list of rising designers, including Galanos, Norell, Trigere, Jean Louis, and, even earlier, Madeleine Vionnet, whom she launched on an illustrious design career in the Roaring Twenties of Paris.

When Carnegie decided to expand her fashion line into jewelry and perfume, her husband, John Zanft, a former vice-president of Fox Studios, headed the perfume industry that bore her name. One of Carnegie's jewelry designers, and also vice-president of the jewelry division, was her nephew, Irving Apisdorf, who worked closely with the manufacturer in the production and design of her signature pieces.

Other designers of Carnegie jewelry included Norman Norell, one of her proteges, and Nadine Effront, a French sculptress and former student of Georges Braque. For the 1963 Carnegie fall collection, Effront designed a line of Greek-inspired pieces, some with tints of verdigris, employing bold and unusual materials like terra cotta, tortoise and hammered gold.

The finished Carnegie pieces created by these and numerous other innovative designers reflected the attention to detail that was her trademark. Many were theme-oriented. Far Eastern and Indian influences are evident in brooches of Oriental figures, an elaborate elephant howdah, and snuff bottle pendants. Another interesting grouping consisted of delightfully outrageous figures - cannibals, animals and fish - fashioned of simulated materials and rumored to be copies of similar pieces of "real" jewelry, originally designed with turquoise, coral and gemstones. If such was indeed true, the exchange was more than fair, for fine jewelry designs were frequently copies of the artistic endeavors of renowned fashion jewelry designers of the era.

Yet there was another side to the Carnegie jewelry lines, reflected in soft, romantic designs - artfully draped crystal and rhinestone necklaces, delicate mother-of-pearl and rhinestone bracelets, and brooches with huge, brilliant stones in rich, vibrant colors. Even a golden apple with pave center where a slice had been removed (possibly symbolizing the Garden of Eden), captures the essence of romanticism, as do the dainty raised-heart earrings, each tiny red stone encapsulated in gold. And, as the *piéce de résistance*, a majestic bison's head, green eye gleaming, bands of rhinestones glimmering at his nostrils and neck, creates an unusual study of powerful beauty.

Grouping of Carnegie brooches. Left to right, 2¼" piece with magnificent green, foil-backed center stone, has antiqued gold tendrils and blue accents, $175-225; a bison's head with gleaming green eye, rhinestone nostrils and collar, $200-300; 3¼" donkey of faux turquoise and coral with rhinestone accents is one design from a grouping of similar figures, animals and fish, $145-185; charming gold donkey with faux moonstone, rhinestone and enamel accents, $85-135.

Elegance abounds in these pieces by Hattie Carnegie.

Left: 3 strands of highly polished red stones with the look of garnets are accented by elaborate gold clasp in this dramatic necklace, $125-175.

Center: large swirling bowls with rhinestone accents form these heavy gold earrings, $60-85; golden apple with slice removed to reveal rhinestone center creates an unusual brooch with a "real" look, $75-125; graceful tendrils fall from large center "carnelian" in this 2¾" x 2¼" brooch, $150-200; woven gold strands encircle a faceted stone with the look of alexandrite, surrounded by clusters of tiny rhinestones, $100-145;

Right: Large, perfect stones create a single strand of eye-catching beauty in this dazzling necklace (only your jeweler knows for sure!), $125-175; marbleized stones intertwine with orange/red beads with large center clasp on this bracelet of changing hues, $100-135.

Three Carnegie Oriental pieces complement an antique Oriental pipe. Left: brooch of figure with bowl and cooking pot, $125-150; center: faux Carnelian snuff bottle on silver chain, $125-150; right: 2¼" elaborate howdah has elephant with accents of pave rhinestones and pearls, $175-250.

17

Three exciting pieces by Hattie Carnegie. Left to right: 2¼" domed brooch of brushed gold and genuine turquoise stones, $150-200; 3½" flower brooch has three genuine quartz stones, with bands of gold intertwining leaves and base, accented by a pearl, $125-175; bracelet features triple row of pink rhinestones flanked by large faux moonstones, $150-200.

Hattie Carnegie died in 1956 at the age of 70, having devoted 59 years to the fashion industry.

Although the Carnegie salon ceased operations in 1965, jewelry and perfume bearing her name continued to be produced, grossing $4 million in the first year of the closing alone. The rights to the Hattie Carnegie jewelry line were sold by the family in the late 1960s to Larry Josephs, who continued the production of Carnegie into the 1970s.

A 1965 newspaper article succinctly summarizes the changing times that once again affected the jewelry industry and the fate of the empire Hattie Carnegie had so carefully built. It stated, "The demise of the Hattie Carnegie salon nine years after the death of its founder, on behalf of corporate enterprises bearing her name, concludes one of America's great success stories and represents the trend to corporate thinking in a field where individuality is fast passing from reality to legend."

Hattie Carnegie was a pioneer in the creation of that legend. Her life of unshakable determination and inspirational achievement is an exciting portrait of accomplishment - and the result of an ultimate belief in the American dream.

Nettie Rosenstein

Vienna, Austria, was also the birthplace of another great couturier. Born Nettie Rosencrans in 1890, her name was later changed to Rosenstein, and at the age of two her family brought her to the United States. Like Carnegie, she also began her career in the millinery field, this time in partnership with her sister.

Rosenstein's prowess in the field of design was recognized early. In 1921 she employed 50 seamstresses, but by 1927, while only in her late 30s, she had already decided to retire. Rosenstein's creativity eventually overrode such a precipitous decision, however, and in 1929 she returned to the fashion world as a designer for Corbet et Cie. But the memory of her past success apparently exerted a magnetic influence, for in 1932 Rosenstein once again established her own house of couture, nurturing it into a million-dollar business in just five short years. Like Carnegie, she also left a generic legacy in the lexicon of couture, for the Rosenstein "little black dress" soon became another symbol of refined and understated elegance in the fashion world.

In 1961, after many years as a brilliant light on Seventh Avenue, Rosenstein decided to discontinue the fashion line that bore her name and concentrate solely on other accessories, including perfume and handbags. Unfortunately, however, Rosenstein jewelry was produced for only a short time thereafter.

According to a New York Times article, she was quoted in 1945 as saying, "I want to see that everything that goes out under my name is right. I'm a perfectionist." And so, when Rosenstein was no longer satisfied that she could control the quality of her garments - and shortly thereafter her jewelry line - she turned her focus elsewhere.

There is no doubt, however, that Rosenstein, like most of her counterparts, was well aware of the value and versatility of accessory items as the final brush stroke in a fashion portrait. She placed great emphasis on their execution, and was not about to compromise when circumstances beyond her control interfered with those standards.

The Rosenstein name was synonymous with the quality that only personal attention can provide, and those attributes are unquestionably apparent in Rosenstein jewelry. They were frequently crafted of sterling silver, some with a fascinating combination of heraldic symbolism and picturesque, romantic images. One piece, which at first glance resembles an elaborate military medal, reveals on closer inspection a cupid being cradled by a protective, yet austere, golden eagle. In another, a cameo is regally placed in the center of a heart-shaped crest with crossed swords, and still another sword is presented with jagged edges, perhaps symbolizing a broken heart.

More traditionally romantic Rosenstein pieces are evident in a sterling silver heart pendant with red crystals emerging from the center; a colorful pansy brooch rimmed with rhinestones; and the soft, pastel stones that create a clocklike effect on a large sterling bracelet. Even a pink rooster

These regal sterling pieces show the artistry and originality to be found in treasures marked Nettie Rosenstein:

clockwise: large sterling cuff bracelet with center clock-like detail in shades of pink and aqua, $250-375; a sterling pink pave rooster struts proudly, $200-275; 2½" sterling pansy clip with rose gold vermeil, rimmed with rhinestones, $225-300; aqua pave stones form the body of this sterling Deco bug with pearl accents and burnished hues, $175-250. All marked Nettie Rosenstein Sterling.

appears decidedly feminine, with its rich enameling and pave stones. One can only speculate as to what further marvels would have reached our hands had Rosenstein been able to continue her supervision of the quality she demanded.

Quality and innovation. It's a marriage that will always have universal appeal to the discerning, fashion-conscious woman. And this diminutive giant, who left Austria as a child and brought with her an indomitable spirit and inspired work ethic, was surely at the forefront of that happy merger. Nettie Rosenstein died in 1980. She was 90 years old.

The jeweler's art in both design and manufacture are well represented in these elaborate Rosenstein pieces:
Left to right: "eagle cradling an angel" (see inset) is a massive sterling piece of intricate detail and beauty (with matching earrings), $600-800; sterling heart pendant with red raised crystals clustered in the center, $150-200; an orange cameo forms the center of this "coat of arms" brooch with crossed swords, $450-600; sterling "broken" sword with elaborate hilt, $175-225.

21

The deep gunmetal grey base and accents of these pieces by Schiaparelli blend with the marble background. Left: Four-piece parure of carved pale green and aurora stones and even paler green pearls is an innovative use of color and design, $750-900. Right top: Similar tones of grey add richness to these pearl and rhinestone earrings, $75-100; blue flowers accented with rhinestones form a delicate pattern in this bracelet of brilliant aurora and crystal stones, again with a gunmetal base, $150-200.

Elsa Schiaparelli

"Two words have always been banned from my house - the word 'creation,' which strikes me as the height of pretentiousness, and the word 'impossible.'"[1]

Thus Elsa Schiaparelli expressed two traits that typified her personality - honest yet artistic expression and strong-willed determination. I will endeavor not to use the word "creation" in relating Elsa Schiaparelli's accomplishments. Surely she did create, and in a most intriguing manner, but we will strive to leave it at that. As for "impossible," it will not be alluded to here, for Schiaparelli's determination and ultimate achievements would never warrant its use!

Elsa Schiaparelli was born in Rome in 1890 to a cultured Italian family. Her uncle was renowned astronomer Giovanni Schiaparelli, who discovered the canals on Mars. Precocious and artistic, her innate abilities surfaced quite early, and even as a child she would not compromise her treasured individuality. At 14 Elsa wrote a book of poems, well beyond her years in scope and content, and it subsequently was published without her parents' knowledge or approval. Shipped off to a convent, she was back home in a mere 90 days, refusing to subjugate her strong personality to the harsh convent disciplines.

As a young woman, marriage took her to New York, but the unhappy union soon faltered and Schiaparelli was left deserted and penniless - with a young daughter to support.

It was these harsh circumstances that forced her to leave the United States for Paris where, with no financing, and only a courageous determination to succeed against what most would have considered overwhelming odds, she soon established the house of couture that would become a beacon of the prewar Parisienne fashion scene. In 1934 Schiaparelli's success enabled her to open another couture house in London, which commanded prestige and popularity but was not as financially successful as its French counterpart across the Channel. One year later, in 1935, she is credited with giving birth to the "boutique" idea, which rapidly spread throughout the world.

Schiaparelli's impeccable sense of fashion, coupled with an exuberant, artistic nature and the courage to present seemingly outrageous innovations in heretofore conventional settings, created a potent and highly successful combination. In her fashion designs, the Schiaparelli purposefulness immediately came to the fore.

In her autobiography Schiaparelli wrote that "...her brain gave out ideas like a fireworks show."[2] And what a show it was! Since she disliked something as basic as buttons, for example, she totally changed them - their size, composition, and design. Using materials like wood, celluloid, jade, china, crystal, and aluminum, she gave buttons a whole new purpose that transcended their simple and somewhat dreary function and transformed them into an eye-catching focal point of the

[1] Schiaparelli, *Shocking Life*, p. 71.

[2] *Ibid.*, p. 81.

23

garment. But perhaps even more important, from gold sovereigns to lollipops, the formerly mundane button now became an artistic and entertaining fashion statement!

Schiaparelli's wittiness was just as apparent in her jewelry - and the "fireworks" continued. Mischievous lapel clips became unlikely containers for fresh flowers, and phosphorescent brooches glowed seductively. Not only did pieces like these open exciting new vistas in costume jewelry, both for the industry and the consumer, but Schiaparelli had the additional courage to feature them on garments that were frequently viewed as stark and somewhat severe. All this from a designer who blossomed into womanhood in the early 20th century, when "imitation jewelry" was generally considered gauche and unacceptable. Obviously, Schiaparelli didn't permit such a sterile attitude to inhibit her individuality. Who else would pin a diamond brooch in the center of a fresh flower, or fashion a clip from the design of fasteners on the coveralls worn by French mechanics! It was, as the French would say, a *feaux d' artifice* - that marvelous combination of "fireworks" and wit!

Like Carnegie and Rosenstein, Schiaparelli, too, left a generic trademark for the industry. In 1936 she featured the dynamic shade that became her signature color. It was "shocking pink" - and shocking pink it remains today.

In 1937 double-clipped earrings bearing the Schiaparelli signature made their debut on the accessory scene and were an immediate success. These showy pieces featured a cluster on top of the ear and another at the lobe. Recently reintroduced, and a forerunner of the multiple ear piercings seen today, it's amazing that Schiaparelli had conceived this "new" idea over a half century before!

Marissa Berenson, famed fashion model, actress and granddaughter of Elsa Schiaparelli, wrote "...Elsa Schiaparelli was a fantastically innovative designer who gave the world embroidered sweaters and jackets, shocking pink and shoulders out to there. More than anything she brought to her work wit and audacity - and great fantasy - that knocked the stuffiness right out of fashion." [3]

Shiaparelli was most certainly a "free thinker" of her generation. Both her clientele and the fashion world were richer for these frank expressions of bold and innovative ideas, and it was indeed fortunate that fashion designers and artists happily joined forces during this exciting time. The results were virtually unparalleled, and Schiaparelli's collaborations proved particularly beneficial.

Pierre Cardin and Hubert de Givenchy began their careers in couture under Schiaparelli's tutelage. Among the designers who contributed to her jewelry repertoire were Lesage, who was responsible for many of her snake-oriented pieces, and Jean Clement, who designed her enameled ivy necklaces. Cecil Beaton - famed photographer and costume designer of theatrical and Hollywood fame (*Gigi, My Fair Lady*) - created Schiaparelli's famous heart clip. Giacomelli designed delightful pieces like lamp posts with cherubs holding the light bulbs, "vegetarian" bracelets, and coins dangling from elaborate dog collar necklaces, as well as fabulous bronze clips that, unfortunately, were too cumbersome to wear with comfort or practicality.

Jean Schlumberger, however, is the jewelry designer most prominently associated with the Schiaparelli name. Considered by many to be one of the modern world's greatest jewelry designers, this young man from Alsace Lorraine began his career using precious and semiprecious stones exclusively. However, he later recognized the challenge of converting these designs to less expensive, but still inherently beautiful, costume pieces. Needless to say, the audience for his talents widened immensely - for Schlumberger had the foresight to include that vast majority of women who otherwise would never have experienced the joy of wearing a Schlumberger creation. It is hardly surprising that he later became vice-president of Tiffany's, with a special department bearing the exclusive Schlumberger name.

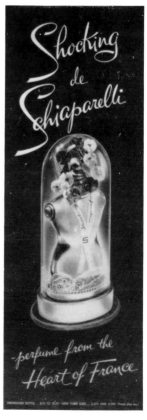

With the advent of World War II, the dangers and restrictions inherent in continuing her enterprises in Paris convinced Schiaparelli to leave her adopted country and return to the United States to fulfill a lecture contract. But, homesick for France, she risked a perilous journey back to Paris in December 1940, only to be forced to make yet another harrowing and courageous departure from her adopted homeland in May of 1941, this time not returning until the war's end in 1945.

[3] Berenson, *Dressing Up*, p. 21.

25

Due to mounting uncertainties, Schiaparelli closed her London house on the eve of the war, but continued to design, especially for Americans and customers in other countries that were still neutral. Unfortunately, although the Paris salon had remained open under the watchful eye of loyal employees during Schiaparelli's absence, it never regained its prewar prominence, as the earth-shattering disruption of half a decade earlier continued to exert powerful repercussions.

In 1954 Schiaparelli decided - as would numerous other designers of this era - to continue her business only in licensed accessory items. For a time prior to and during this period, Schiaparelli jewelry was produced by the illustrious U.S. firm of De Rosa, also renowned for costume pieces bearing their own name. However, the Schiaparelli jewelry line was discontinued only a few years after her 1954 decision.

Elsa Schiaparelli died in Paris in 1973 at the age of 83. The contributions of Schiaparelli and her distinguished colleagues remain entrenched in the annals of fashion and accessory design - and her own personal sense of style continues to leave an undeniable imprint. It is seen every day in the choices of a multitude of daring yet fashionably attuned women who also assert their individuality by the use of bold accessories.

As Marissa Berenson recalled, "My grandmother was petite and always wore masses of jewelry. And big things - big brooches, bracelets, big rings. Lots of everything!"[4]

"There are lots of things in this world that one has to be serious about. I don't think dressing up is one of them. Dressing up is about fun...and glamour - and being a little creative with yourself!"[5]

[4] *Ibid.*, p. 69.

[5] *Ibid.*, p. 69.

A Schiaparelli design combines both whimsy and imaginative elegance. This 3" bar brooch resembles a Faberge egg with its marbleized back and glittering stones in an unusual shade of green covering the front, $200-300.

Top to bottom: Faux watermelon tourmalines encircle this classic necklace by Schiaparelli, $250-350; from the same genre, a brilliant tourmaline-look brooch and earrings, $225-300; pink stones and pearls create a feminine combination in this brooch, with convenient pendant hook, and matching swirl earrings, $350-450.

Top to bottom: Burnished gold brooch with black stones and rim of rhinestones has a classic look, yet is highly detailed, $150-225; large cluster earrings of multi-shape and size, $85-125; overlapping gold tendrils encase a huge topaz colored stone in this exciting brooch, $125-175; bold "cover the ear" earrings of brilliant citrine-colored stones need nothing more to make heads turn! $150-200. The sleek, double leaf brooch can also be worn as a pendant, $65-85.

From a private collection, the varied pieces on pages 28-31 are valued from $500 to $4000.

G. "Coco" Chanel

The mystique that was and is "Coco" Chanel was clarified in a most succinct manner by Jean Cocteau when he wrote, "She has by a kind of miracle, worked in fashion according to rules that would seem to have value for painters, musicians, poets."[6]

Born in France in 1883 and later orphaned and raised in a convent, Gabrielle Chanel subconsciously embraced those rules by absorbing the sights around her during these early years, an ability that would separate her time and again from the masses. When she opened her house of couture as a young woman in 1914, many of those images would reappear in her designs. "Even before the Twenties, she had begun to make her indelible mark by being first to recognize the twentieth century for what it is...and dressing women accordingly."[7]

Her garments frequently reflected an uncommon ability to convert a basically masculine look - harkening back to the uniform of schoolboys from her convent years - into fashions with a feminine quality. Most especially she remembered the black smocks and their collars with the floppy bow ties. "And so for half a century a certain suit...adorned with the same collar and the same tie, went trotting through the streets of Europe and the two Americas. It was a worldwide bestseller...."[8]

A trendsetter and unabashed individualist, Chanel's designs frequently matched her own distinctively gaminlike quality. In fact, she was credited with introducing the suntanned look, which was immediately embraced by untold numbers of women who had heretofore treasured their pale and carefully protected skin.

Chanel's daring ideas were perfect for the early days of Hollywood and led to a short-lived and unsatisfactory stint with Goldwyn in 1931. Who knows what other fanciful trends might have been embraced by American women of the Depression years - who were undoubtedly hungry for a touch of glamour - had her experience on the Hollywood scene been a more pleasant one!

Never resenting the blatant copies of her easily recognizable designs, Chanel instead embraced the old saying, "Imitation is the sincerest form of flattery." By 1938 her fame had spread worldwide, and she employed 4,000 people at locations throughout the United States, Canada, Europe and Asia. Obsessed with her birth date, August 5, Chanel made certain that all her important openings only occurred on the 5th of the month. Introduced in 1923, even Chanel No. 5, the ultimate source of her wealth, was purportedly connected to her birth date.

[6] Cocteau, *Harper's Bazaar*, March 1954, p. 168.

[7] *Ibid.*

[8] Charles-Roux, *Chanel*, p. 53.

Twice Chanel was forced to close the doors of her Paris salon. In 1914, shortly after opening her first shop, the First World War interrupted her efforts. As it had for many other designers, World War II also proved Chanel's temporary undoing, although the second hiatus was a longer and more costly one - both psychologically and physically. This time her doors were closed in 1939 and - partly because of a scandal involving her alleged association with a German during the occupation - Chanel wisely chose not to reenter the fashion scene until 1954.

Her timing was impeccable, for women were once again ready for Chanel's "easy" fashions as an alternative to the "new look" of 1947, which had, by then, run its course. Although these casual designs received cool reviews from the European press, their success was immediate in the United States. Her contributions were not lost on fellow countrymen like Jean Cocteau, however. For when she reopened her salon at 31 Rue Cambon in 1954, and presented her first collection in 15 years, he wrote, "Her return...represents far more than the reopening of a great *maison de couture*...she arrives as a sign that we must vanquish the inflation of mediocrity. Her instinct does not deceive her."[9]

The popularity of the basic Chanel look continued, and it endures today - a classic style that has more than proven its staying power in a constantly changing industry. The pink suit Jacqueline Kennedy wore on that fateful day in Dallas was by Chanel. And thus, Chanel designs have left an indelible impact through tragic times, as well - and a stark pictorial reminder for the history books.

Chanel is credited with playing a major role in the introduction of "fashion" jewelry by having the foresight to make copies of her own "real" pieces, "...so that," as she said, "women can wear fortunes that cost nothing."[10] Like Schiaparelli, her flair for bold jewelry with conservative outfits changed the look of accessorizing for many adventuresome women. With sweaters and classic daywear, for instance, she showed elaborate pieces usually considered only appropriate for evening.

[9] *Harper's Bazaar*, p. 168.

[10] Carter, *Magic Names in Fashion*, p. 55.

Although Chanel was at the forefront of the trend toward costume jewelry, she also designed diamond pieces for the International Guild of Diamond Merchants, an unlikely collaboration, since she had previously expressed a preference for only colored stones and pearls. Her diamond designs included jewelry that could be converted into separate pieces (e.g., Eisenberg, p. 75). Another was called the Chanel fringe - bangs of diamonds in strands across the forehead! When Chanel conceived these pieces for a charity showing, she had no problem understanding this side of jewelry design, for she had garnered many workable ideas for costume pieces by her association with the wealthy and their "real" gems.

In addition to her own contributions, Count Etienne de Beaumont, who started with Chanel in the 1920s, was responsible for many of her jewelry designs, and Fulco Santostefano della Cerda, Duke of Verdura, contributed others after he joined her in 1927 as a textile designer.

Karl Lagerfeld's fall 1989 and spring 1990 collections for the house of Chanel clearly emphasized the importance he, too, placed on accessories as an adjunct to the incomparable *Chanel look* - gold chains and necklaces elaborately draped over the shoulders, multi-jeweled chains at the waist, and giant clips caught seductively in soft folds at the hip dramatically complemented his fall 1989 line. The introduction of Lagerfeld's spring 1990 fashions - heralding an auspicious entrance into this century's new but final decade - also featured an array of dazzling jewelry, including stunning variations on the classic Chanel pearls, along with bold, multi-stoned brooches and dynamic earrings, many resplendent with huge, colorful cabochons.

These, and later, Chanel entrants are a tribute to the philosophy of design that has been the hallmark of Chanel's posthumous fashion message to women everywhere, a message as flawless today as it was over a half century ago!

In 1978, only seven short years after Chanel's death, Christie's in London auctioned her costume jewelry, fetching prices comparable to those of precious gems and gold - indeed a tribute to the respect and awe the Chanel name continues to inspire.

Photograph Courtesy of Dorothy Torem.

Back in 1954 Cocteau wrote of her, "We are happy to see, advancing over the marshes where our pride has been somewhat stagnant, the marvelous little head of a black swan. It belongs to Mademoiselle Chanel...."[11]

This dramatic image of Coco Chanel remains intact as we enter the twenty-first century - the "black swan" who continues to influence the face of design. For her fashion legacy is, and will undoubtedly remain, timeless.

[11] *Harper's Bazaar*, p. 168.

Earrings of multi-red stones in a random design, marked Bijoux Christian Dior 1959, $50-75; dainty gold and rhinestone earrings with lustrous red cabochons fool the eye with their expensive look of precious gems and 14K gold, marked Christian Dior, with patent number, $40-60; 1½" rhinestone earrings accented with pastel, heart-shaped flowers, marked Christian Dior, $85-125. Layered rose in burnished silver forms a captivating brooch, marked Dior, Germany, 1974, $125-175; long rope of gold with delicate rhinestone spacers also creates the elegant look of precious jewelry, marked Chr. Dior, Germany, 1973, $95-135.

Christian Dior

Born in France in 1905, Dior's initial career was that of an art dealer. After World War II, however, his path changed direction, and he found what was undoubtedly his true niche in the world of artistic endeavor: fashion design. After several apprenticeships, he shot to stardom with his premiere showing at the House of Dior in 1947.

After the restrictions and austerity of wartime France, postwar Parisians were understandably eager for a return to exciting new directions in the field of couture. Even though upscale women's magazines in the United States had continued to show elegant and glamourous images, fashion choices were restrictive for much of the population on both sides of the Atlantic. With the end of World War II, couture was understandably ripe for dramatic changes both here and abroad.

Inherently sensing the need for a fashion revolution to accompany this new era of peace and prosperity, Dior was first out of the starting gate with a radical concept that was in sharp contrast to what had gone before. Hitting the fashion runway in 1947, it was appropriately christened the "New Look" -- and *new* it was! With huge, full skirts that fell just 12 inches from the floor and accentuated the waistline, the "New Look" became an overnight success in Europe and the United States, ushering in a transcendent, post-war cycle that changed fashion history -- and ensured Dior's place in it!

Tragically, Dior was to live only ten years beyond this spectacular success. He died in 1957 while only in his 50s. His licensed items, including jewelry, continued to be produced. Some exceptionally beautiful examples of Dior jewelry were made in the United States by Kramer in the 1950s, and these pieces are marked Dior by Kramer. Most of Dior's jewelry during this "golden age" period, however, was produced in West Germany by Grosse and Maer, and is marked Dior, West Germany, and dated. Incidentally, designs bearing only the Grosse designation are of fine quality and a worthwhile addition to any costume jewelry collection.

It is clear that the production of Dior jewelry, from the period preceding as well as following his untimely death, was predicated on continuing the essence of glamour that will always be synonymous with the Dior image.

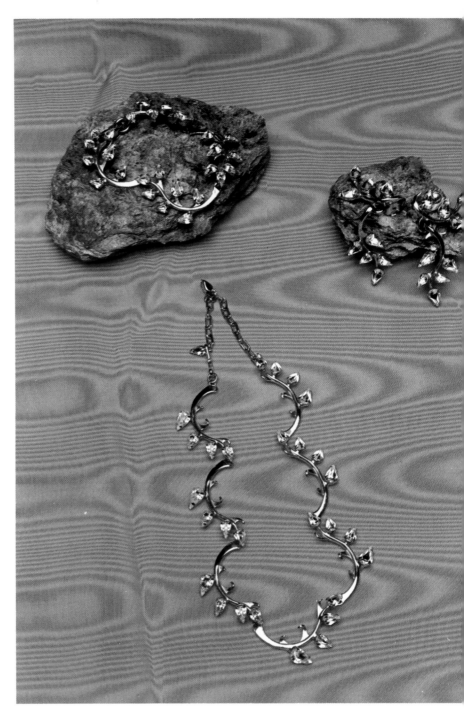

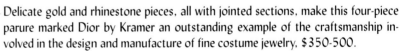

Delicate gold and rhinestone pieces, all with jointed sections, make this four-piece parure marked Dior by Kramer an outstanding example of the craftsmanship involved in the design and manufacture of fine costume jewelry, $350-500.

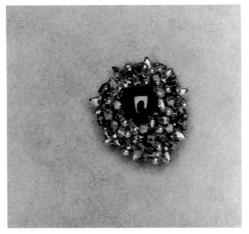

This brooch is an elaborate cluster of faux amber, citrines and pearls, with an onyx-like center. Marked Dior Germany, it is attributable to either Grosse or Maer, $125-175.

Exquisite workmanship and attention to detail are unmistakable in this four-piece parure with many intricate sections, marked Dior by Kramer, $650-900. Leather handbag, labeled Dior, Paris, has rigid handle studded with large, brilliant crystals, $450-650.

Synthetic cabochons in multi-colors and shapes are nestled in this elaborate necklace of layered leaves and scrollwork marked Yves Saint Laurent 300/500, and initialed YSL at bottom. A rare Parisienne runway piece, $1800+.

Yves Saint Laurent

Yves Saint Laurent was born in Algeria in 1936 to French parents. He became an apprentice with Dior at the age of 18, and a mere three years later, after the death of Dior in 1957, assumed responsibility for the line. Saint Laurent was also a great admirer of Chanel. Usually grudging in her praise, she returned his admiration, at one time considering him her logical successor.

Saint Laurent's first showing after Dior's death was "...a production in the finest Dior tradition of exquisite finish and a perfect marriage of accessories. (It was later to be seen that Saint Laurent needed no lessons in accessorizing)."[12]

The first collection under the aegis of his own house appeared in 1962. Three years later, the YSL enterprises became part of Lanvin-Charles of the Ritz, and Saint Laurent departed on an entirely new venture, signaling his entrance into the "ready-to-wear" market: the YSL/Rive Gauche boutiques. The first Boutique opened in Paris in 1966, and by 1979 the Rive Gauche name had expanded to 160 similar operations worldwide.

This highly successful venture gives credence to the depth of Saint Laurent's belief in the intrinsic value of accessorizing, and that he was "...at heart an inspired boutique designer who could transform a familiar shape by means of imaginative accessories."[13]

In addition to his fashion leadership, the YSL griffe eventually encompassed more than 50 products including jewelry, which continues to be available in his boutiques. His feelings about the importance of accessories match those of many other fashion mavens. "Yves is almost jealous of the accessory designers saying that they have more creative freedom than designers of clothes because the choice of materials in handbags and jewelry is as wide as anyone can wish for."[14] In 1976 Saint Laurent said, "Accessories are extremely important today. They have become almost more important than clothes."[15]

In the 1970s Saint Laurent frequently called upon the Schiaparelli look of decades before, making them his own by molding their somewhat angular lines to a more contemporary, softer silhouette.

And so, Saint Laurent's talents - not unlike those of his predecessors and contemporaries - happily reflect his own unique individualism and daring, and also the influence of other designers and mentors - from Chanel to Dior to Schiaparelli.

Cartier is the American licensee for Yves Saint Laurent jewelry in the United States.

[12] Carter, *Magic Names*, p. 195.

[13] *Ibid.*, p. 199.

[14] Madsen, *Living for Design - The Yves Saint Laurent Story*, p. 57.

[15] Carter, *Magic Names*, p. 199.

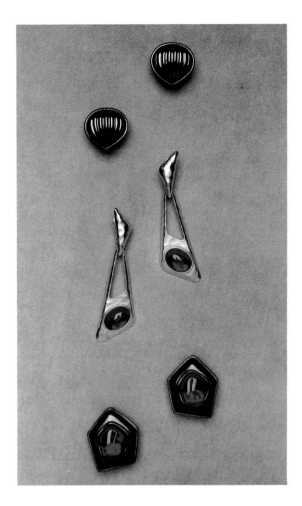

Three pair of Yves Saint Laurent earrings. Top and bottom pieces have stunning gunmetal finishes, with bottom pair featuring large "jelly" red stones, top, $40-50; bottom, $65-85; center pair are of hammered gold with red cabachons, $100-150.

This 2¼" Deco style Givenchy brooch has a brilliant foiled center stone and black enamel accents. Earrings are equally impressive. $250-300 set.

Givenchy

Influenced by Balenciaga, Hubert de Givenchy began his career in 1945, working with Lelong and Jacque Fath. From 1949 to 1951 he designed for Schiaparelli and opened his own house in 1952. His clothing and accessories are sold worldwide through Novelle Boutiques.

Cabochon stones of deep amber red are surrounded by gold filigree in these dramatic 2¾" earrings, marked Givenchy, $100-150.

Heavy gold links with center swirls of pave rhinestones create a bold choker and matching bracelet marked Givenchy, $300-400.

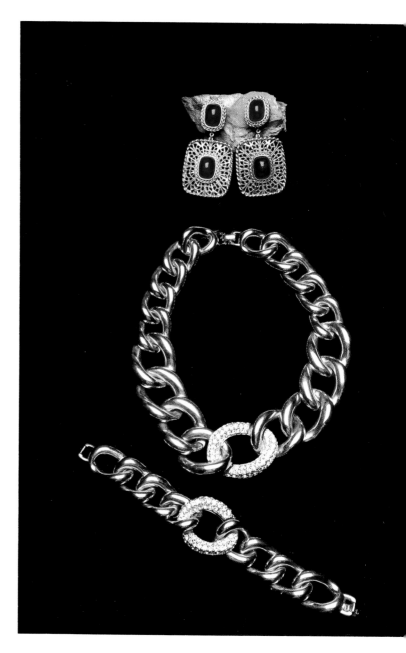

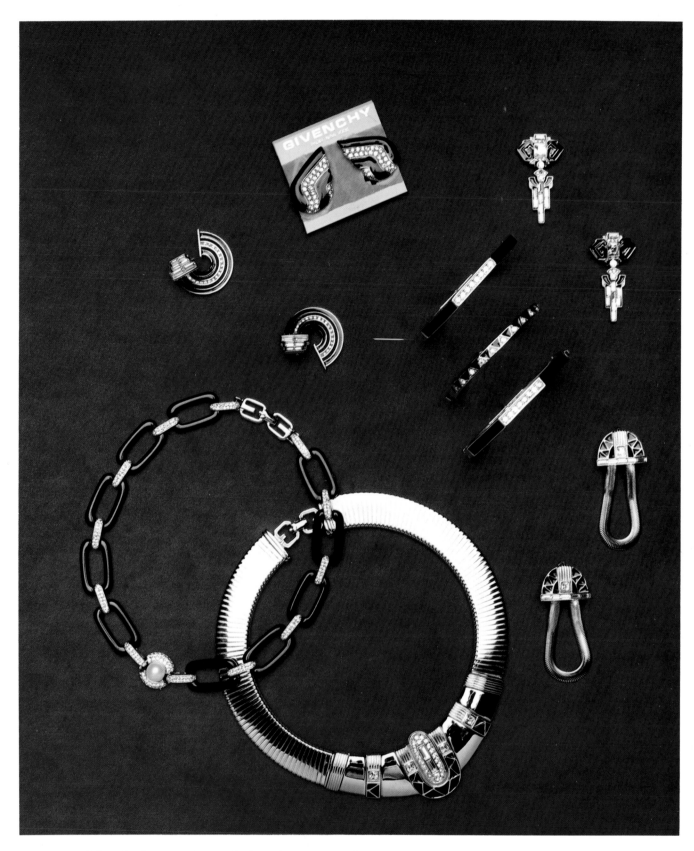

A feast for the eyes and a treat for Deco devotees, these Givenchy pieces all reflect striking black and rhinestone Deco designs. Link necklace, $150-175; Bib necklace, $275-375; Earrings top center, $65-85; Earrings top left, $85-100; Earrings top right, $85-100; Bracelets, $125-150 ea.; Earrings bottom right, $125-175.

Opposite:
These tailored, frequently logo-inspired pieces are indicative of the delicate designs and fine workmanship common to Pierre Cardin jewelry. Rope necklace, $75-100; Earrings, $30-50; Stickpins, $45-60 ea.

Cardin

Born in Italy in 1922, Pierre Cardin worked for both Schiaparelli and Dior in Paris before establishing his own house there in 1950. Cardin has been at the forefront of innovative ideas in fashion. He is considered the founder of the unisex trend, and was a primary force behind the introduction of accessory items for men.

Cardin also designed accessory lines that were exclusively made for his French couture showings. However, they were frequently adapted for jewelry sold under the Cardin name by New York licensee, Swank, Inc.

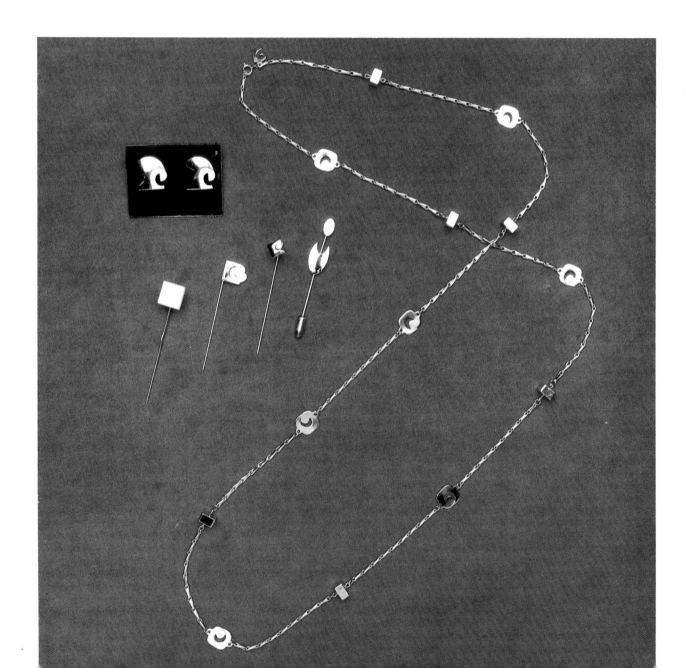

Adele Simpson

Adele Simpson was born in New York City in 1903. She began her career in couture in 1925, and in 1944 founded the company bearing her name. The Adele Simpson label has always been a symbol of quality and consistency on the American fashion scene.

An adjunct to other offerings like perfume, Simpson's jewelry was only produced for a short period during the 1950s. She worked closely with the manufacturers in the production of this new line, with all adhering to the same quality standards she demanded when bringing her fashion designs to fruition. Offered in exclusive shops like Joseph Magnin, Simpson's jewelry even then commanded prices of $50 to $500 each and was enormously popular. A piece of jewelry marked with her signature is a coup for collectors today, since it is rarely found.

Rarely found in costume jewelry, Adele Simpson logo appears on this 2½" Sterling vermeil brooch with cluster of amber and rhinestones. A truly unique piece. $400-500.

42

Anne Klein

A native New Yorker, Anne Klein's artistic abilities were recognized early, when she was awarded a scholarship in high school to continue her education in the study of fashion. In what could possibly be interpreted as innate intuition, she decided to pursue freelance fashion sketching instead, and this bold decision started her on the path that led to astounding success in a field that was, and remains, highly competitive.

Among her innovations was the establishment of the young-junior concept in fashion design, which changed the previously fussy, "little girl" image of junior fashions into garments of sleek simplicity and sophistication. This revolutionary step became a hallmark of Anne Klein's philosophy of design, both in fashion and accessories.

By 1968, Anne Klein and her husband, Matthew Rubinstein, along with two partners, had established Anne Klein and Company and Anne Klein Studio, later affiliating with the American arm of a Japanese company in order to better distribute and produce their repertoire of fashion items on an international scale.

Recipient of the Coty Hall of Fame award on three separate occasions, Anne Klein was also the only designer to twice receive the prestigious Neiman-Marcus Award.

Although she died in 1974 at the age of 51, Anne Klein's accomplishments and contributions to the fashion world are enormous and, under the mantle of designer Louis Dell'Olio, and others during the ensuing years, the company she founded continues as a highly successful force on the fashion scene.

Dell'Olio and Anne Klein were both born in the sign of Leo - explaining the distinctive lion's head Anne Klein logo - and he maintained the same philosophy of fashion that became the cornerstone of Anne Klein's own individuality. His advocacy of good style as opposed to fashion per se epitomized Klein's credo that although fashions come and go, good style is forever, for *style* gives women an opportunity to express their own individuality, while *fashion* frequently dictates instead of leads.

Since 1981, jewelry bearing the Anne Klein name has been manufactured under license by Swank, Inc. in their Attleboro, Massachusetts, facilities. Swank has been a mainstay in the jewelry industry for more than 100 years. Following the pattern that Anne Klein had adopted, their designers continue to maintain a sense of synchronicity between the accessory and fashion lines, one complementing the other.

As an adjunct to the regular Anne Klein jewelry line, the exclusive Anne Klein Couture Collection is also produced, and is designed to coordinate with the runway fashions. Additionally, the jewelry-type buttons that are frequently an important feature of Anne Klein garments are manufactured with the same care as the Couture Collection.

Anne Klein jewelry, from the past as well as the present, is timeless and classic, and follows the tradition she meticulously established in the production of her garments. The astrological Leo continues to maintain his watchful eye over this mainstay of the fashion and jewelry industry!

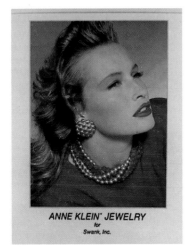

ANNE KLEIN° JEWELRY
for
Swank, Inc.

Bold earrings and bead necklace by Anne Klein Jewelry, New York.

Other Names to Look For

GEORGIO ST. ANGELO   MARY McFADDEN
LILY DACHE   JEAN PATOU
JAMES GALANOS   PAULINE TRIGERE
MR. JOHN

This unsigned choker and earrings parure is the art of enameling at its finest. Along with the flowers, tiny stones and an unusual color combination add a touch of the Orient to its unusual design. $95-135

Costume Jewelry Mania

Synthetics on parade! Top left: Bakelite goes sophisticated with this daring red cigarette holder, $125-175; top right: a 4" brooch of Bakelite pea pods is brimming with a crop of lustrous pearl "peas," $350-500; the center bracelet has a bar clasp and a bounty of clustered, candy-like fruit, $175-250; at bottom left is a bar brooch of luscious Bakelite cherries with green leaves, $175-225.

This unmarked bracelet with luminous "confetti" links is of the lightweight material frequently substituted for heavier metals during and following World War II. It remains shiny and new in spite of its age. A nostalgic glimpse of the past. $125-175.

With apologies to Dickens, "It was the best of times, it was the worst of times." However, the best far outweighed the worst when the costume jewelry boom was in full flower during the 1940s through the 1960s, for the "worst" was simply an excess of the best - a silver lining of sorts!

Indeed it was not lack of demand that made it so, for the demand far exceeded what most manufacturers and designers could realistically meet. It was primarily for this reason that many exceptional pieces reached the hands of eager buyers with no manufacturer's mark or signature, and why many present-day collectors and dealers are puzzled and frustrated when they discover a truly outstanding piece of costume jewelry without an identifying mark.

It was also an exasperating decade because certain metals were almost exclusively relegated for World War II defense-related purposes and not to meet the overwhelming demands of American women for modestly priced jewelry to adorn their clothing during the post-Depression era. Jobs were no longer at a premium, money was flowing more freely, and women yearned to recover from the drab years that preceded World War II by upgrading their fashion image. Just how serious women were in their quest for accessorizing is evidenced by the fact that, despite the shortages, jewelry sales in 1943 were 30 percent higher than they had been in 1941 - due in no small measure to the ingenuity of an industry that would not allow this unprecedented surge of interest in their product to go unfulfilled.

Always innovative, jewelry manufacturers and designers valiantly tried to "keep up" - first, of course, by using the supplies already on hand, including base metals and in some cases sterling silver, and then by working with synthetics to create unusual new designs. The result was a very unique 1940s costume look, especially at what was then the lower end of the jewelry spectrum. Lightweight materials, sometimes paper-based but with a distinctly metallic look, appeared in abundance. Surprisingly, these pieces have weathered the test of time remarkably well. Successor to the ever-popular Bakelite pieces of the 1930s with their whimsical designs, synthetics - some peppered with confettilike glitter and insets of color - remain delightfully capricious and, along with their "kissin' cousin" Bakelite, eminently collectible.

In fact, the use of these materials continued into the following decades as well, encompassing other designs, many quite elaborate. And, in various forms, they flourish today in elegant and expensive pieces - like huge acrylic bracelets and lucite watches - that utilize the versatility of these synthetics by crafting them in very innovative ways.

Many beautiful designs were produced during wartime as well, reflecting the stylish Deco look that abounded in the 1920s and 1930s. From heavy sterling fur clips, studded with large, brilliant stones in graceful settings, to intricately tiered pieces of elaborate construction and bold color combinations, they served as an introduction to the designs of the 1950s and 1960s, as the costume jewelry industry continued its upward spiral.

Even military insignias and medals from this and the prior period have made their way into the lexicons of modern jewelry. However, history reveals that for females to wear them is not a new idea. In fact, they were used as a decorative accessory by Elizabeth of Russia in the sixteenth century and in an amusingly functional manner by her daughter Empress Anna. Whenever she spotted her dress, the Empress simply added another order, and was soon weighed down by medal after medal in a valiant attempt to disguise the evidence of her faulty table manners!

Although the late Diana Vreeland had discovered after the close of World War II that these insignias made a bold fashion statement - and were fun, as well - widespread interest in them didn't really surface until Sotheby's 1987 auction of her jewelry collection. Included were European military medals that she had "discovered" after World War II and worn in groupings on whatever struck her fancy. Diana Vreeland is quoted as saying, "One day the Duchess of Windsor saw me wearing all of them. She told me, 'Diana, stand there. I want David to look at you.' Then she said, 'David, why can't I look like Diana?'"[1] And so, many American women have chosen to emulate Ms. Vreeland's impeccable sense of fashion "know-how" and originality - and accomplish a look that even the Duchess of Windsor envied - in a rather unusual and exciting way!

It seems no more than fitting that this interest by women in an art form long appreciated by militaria collectors has brought about renewed appreciation of the works of these unheralded artisans of military and fraternal insignias - distinguished jewelry designers in their own right - as their elaborate and painstaking workmanship adorns the jackets, coats, sweaters and hats of many contemporary women.

The postwar years saw a steady increase in costume jewelry's popularity. The economy continued its upward spiral, and an air of frivolity accompanied the new trends in fashion and accessorizing. Like the Roaring Twenties, it was

time for fun once again, and jewelry designs reflected that sense of playfulness.

[1] Talley, Fanfair, *Vanity Fair*, October 1987.

Foreign military medals representing Spain, Bulgaria and Serbia. Diana Vreeland recognized their outstanding artistic value, as well as their accessorizing potential, and added this category of military adornment to her fashion legacy.

The Art Moderne influence was also very evident and presented a delightful contrast to its showier counterparts. With its uncluttered, bold designs, this somewhat geometric yet angular look, frequently with combinations of florentine and polished gold and silvertone finishes, gained a popularity of its own.

Thus, the needs of postwar women were met. The more tailored yet conspicuous Art Moderne designs contrasted sharply with the glitter and glitz, and both combined to present costume jewelry that had wide appeal for women of all tastes. Little wonder that, as the decades of the 1940s, 1950s, and 1960s rolled along, the manufacturers could barely keep up with their orders as the demands increased.

However, in the early 1970s the costume jewelry industry came to a crisis point - one from which many designers and manufacturers would never recover. Suddenly, there was an upsurge of interest in gold, probably prompted - at least to some extent - by the steady increase in gold prices on the world market. Many American women erroneously believed that owning and wearing the most insignificant of simple gold chains would somehow be a wise investment, and this shift caused an unprecedented upheaval in the industry.

Charm bracelets are enjoying a much deserved revival, and this unmarked beauty, probably from the 1950s or 1960s, has intriguing baubles to compliment its heavy gold chain, $200-250.

This grouping of pins reflects the playful attitude of jewelry that could be purchased for a pittance in most "five and dimes" before, during, and for several years after the war years of the 1940s. $15-35 each.

48

There were, of course, that ever-present and vast number of women who refused to be tied to a fashion statement that was, for the most part, not a statement at all. Indeed, the statement was - at least for them - mute! They felt that unless one had enough money to purchase jewelry with heavy links of 14-carat gold, or bold and elaborate pieces with gold and gemstones, few outfits would be complemented by what could only be referred to as a smattering of "ditzy" gold chains, barely discernable to the eye. But, unfortunately, enough women chose the path of insignificant gold pieces to send the industry reeling.

Many illustrious names - both designers and manufacturers - were financially unable to continue, and others, who had already devoted decades to their business, opted to retire and not wait for the inevitable swing back. And swing back it did, as evidenced by the fact that many of those artisans from the earlier days, along with their younger counterparts, continued to weave their magic through the 1980s and beyond.

Three examples of the skilled workmanship and appealing designs to be found in many unmarked pieces. The cobra cuff bracelet at top is studded with huge green stones of varying shapes and shades, $125-150; center bracelet showcases a multitude of frosted, wrapped, and gold-capped stones, $150-175; at bottom is a linked bracelet of pastel enameled flowers with rhinestone centers, $125-150. All involve considerable mastery of the jewelers' art.

A 3" brooch of the mythological Zeus graphically illustrates the imaginative and unabashed beauty that can be achieved in the designers' and jewelers' art. Unmarked, its value nevertheless remains intact, for this piece can stand on its own. $325-375.

These sterling pieces with no designer marks, including graceful birds, stylized Deco designs, a whimsical jelly belly and a crown that departs from the style made popular by Trifari and Coro, are examples of beautiful, high quality pieces that are well worth adding to any collection. Green swan, $150-175; Frog, $225-300; Deco bug, $125-150; Gold and red brooch, $175-225; Bird, $150-175; Bee, $100-125; Crown, $175-225.

This unmarked 3¼" brooch of pink-toned sterling vermeil is a captivating mix of unusual styling and interesting stones and colors to complement the rhinestone accents, $175-250.

This trio of sterling brooches is a fine example of the quality and beauty to be found in many pieces without designer marks. At the top is a graceful flower in pink-toned vermeil with faux amethyst center, $200-275. The 4" trumpet flower at left is stunningly detailed in design and execution, $375-500. The brooch at right, with its cupped flowers of multiple red stones, maintains a delicate aura even though it measures a lofty 4½" x 3½", $175-225.

Manufacturers at Work

The following pages are a tribute to all the individuals, both in the forefront and behind the scenes, whose artistry and daring made the "golden years" such and exciting time - not only in the industry itself, but also for American women who were determined to make a statement with their accessories without spending a veritable fortune to do so.

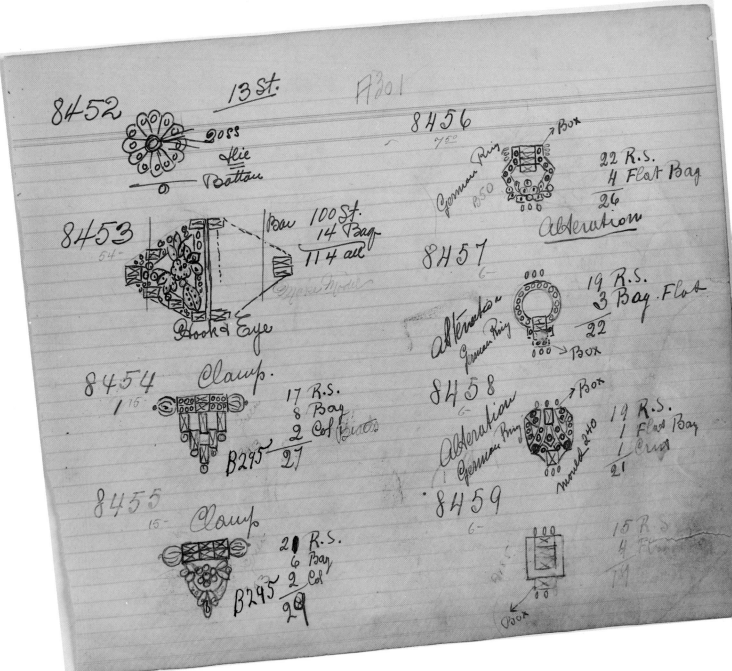

The designs came first, c. 1930. Courtesy Polcini archives.

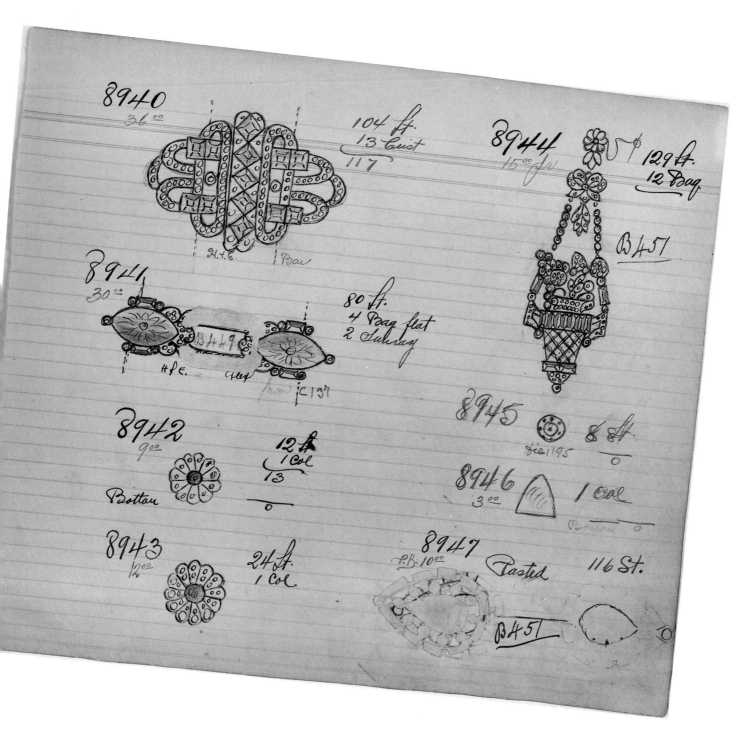

Many other delicate procedures are necessary for jewelry making to evolve from the initial design to a finished product. These Ralph Polcini design drawings from the 1930s are a lasting tribute to his artistry. Courtesy of the Polcini family.

53

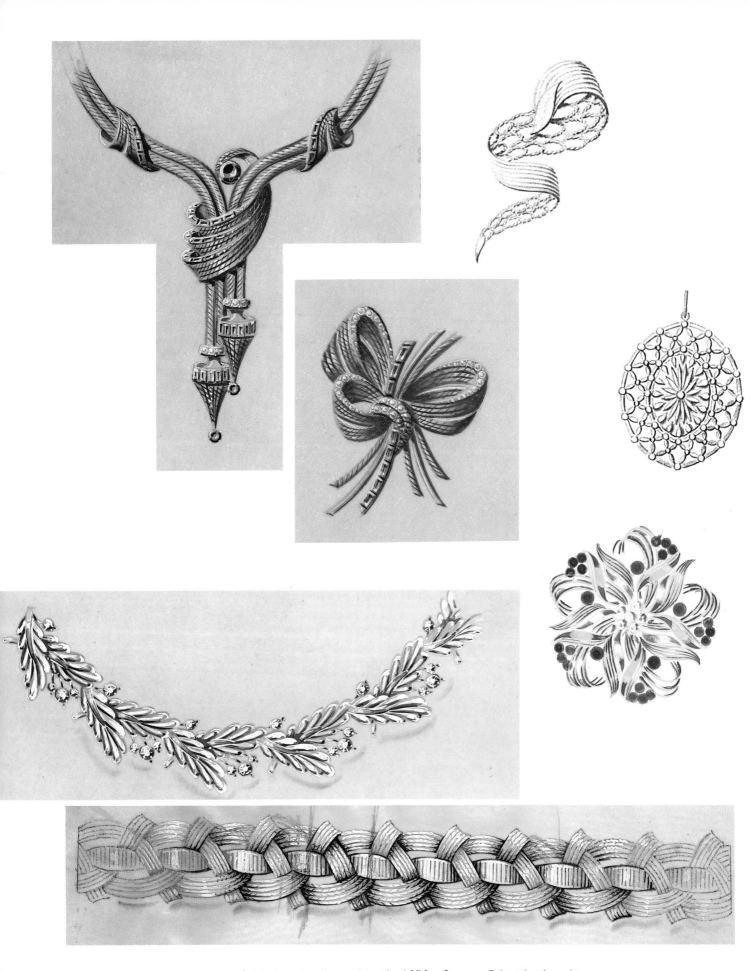

Original jewelry designs from the 1950s. Courtesy Polcini family archives.

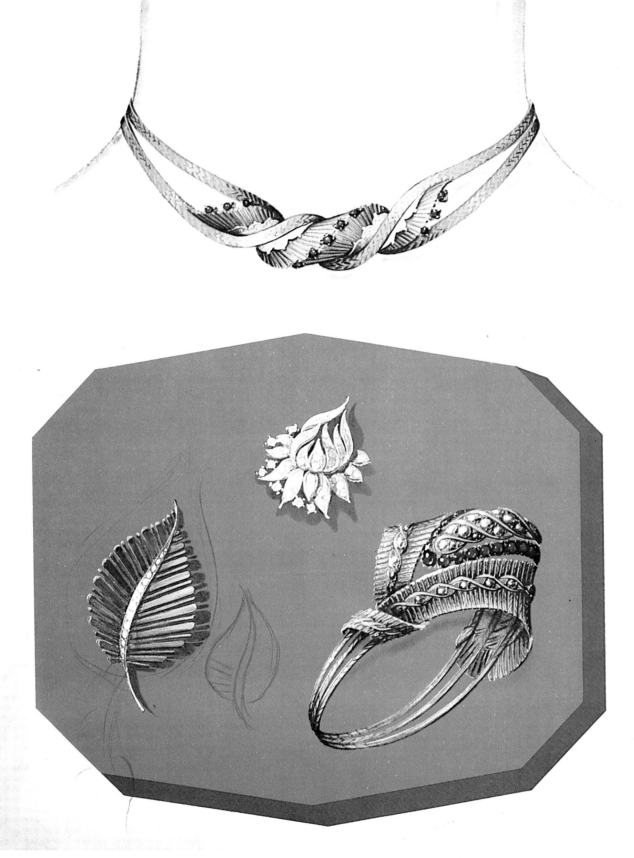

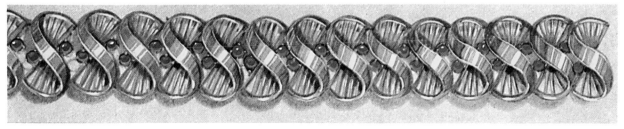

Modelmakers, stone setters, die cutters, and engravers, epoxy experts, chain makers and those responsible for the final inspection all contribute their expertise before each piece is proudly displayed in the manufacturer's showroom or salesman's jewelry case.

Die cutting and engraving. The author's father at work in the 1930s.

Forging pendants and chains in preparation for plating. Courtesy Joan Castle Joseff.

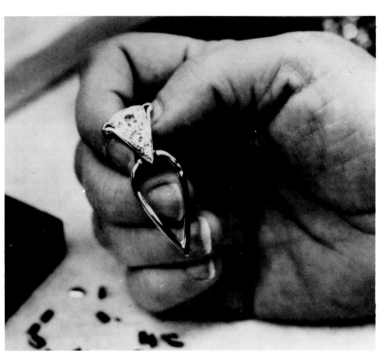

Each stone is carefully positioned by hand using fine tweezers. Courtesy Monet archives.

Color epoxy is inserted into a syringe and then hand applied by a skilled worker to the appropriate surface areas on the jewelry. Courtesy Monet archives.

Necklace with pendant in the process of plating. Courtesy Joan Castle Joseff.

Necklaces are finished when their stones are set in place.

Bi-metal chains are produced by patiently hand twisting fine rhodium around a gold plated rope chain. The ends are then carefully finished together using fine wire and tweezers. Courtesy Monet archives.

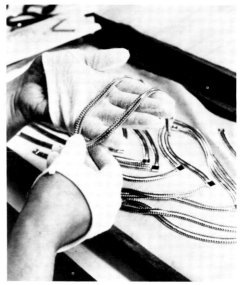

Jewelry is carefully inspected after each stage of its manufacture. Courtesy Monet archives.

57

When you want to buy jewelry, you should first know how much you want to spend. Then be guided by the type of clothes you wear, and where you wear them.

If you want to acquire a collection, start with a brooch because you will find most use for it. It can be pinned on a suit lapel, collar or pocket...or a hat, a belt, or an evening gown. Remember, gold can be worn with more things than silver and topaz is a good stone that looks smart with almost every type of costume....

Earrings should be the next jewelry investment. They also have many uses. You can wear them on your hat, cuffs, shoes, as well as on your ears.

A ring comes next in your collection and I'd suggest finding a bold ring with a large stone...something massive and distinctive.

A bracelet and a necklace come last in importance because they can so seldom be worn with all your costumes or for all occasions.

Keep in mind the fact that jewelry is an accent that draws the eye. With a necklace, earrings and hat or hair ornament, the eye is forced to encircle the face. If you have lovely hands, a bracelet or ring will draw attention to them. A belt buckle, or a pin worn at the waistline, will make people notice a slender waist. Put a pair of buckles on your slippers if you want people to see your small feet.

Just be careful to keep the one important piece of jewelry in one area, to focus attention there. Otherwise, if you use too much jewelry in a scattered way, the eye zig-zags without getting any particular impression.

We follow these principles when we place jewelry in a store window. We can put fifty pieces in a window in such a way that the eye will start at one point, go around the case and finally focus on one particular item.

From an article by Joseff, *Movie Show*, February 1948.

From Joseff archives, courtesy of Joan Castle Joseff.

60

The art of jewelry design was not confined to New York City and Providence, Rhode Island, for the aura of Hollywood surrounded one of the most prolific and innovative of this elite group. His name was Eugene Joseff, and he earned a place in the annals of jewelry design as *Joseff of Hollywood*.

Designer of much of the outstanding jewelry worn by top stars both on- and offscreen during Hollywood's heyday, it was indeed prophetic that the "golden ages" of movies and costume jewelry coincided. Both were magic! One was the fantasy of the silver screen. The other was the fantasy that Joseff wove when his magnificent designs adorned the costumes worn by gorgeous women and swashbuckling heroes in hundreds of epic films.

Born in Chicago, Joseff claimed he was expelled from every school he attended. However, his later achievements would certainly belie his supposed lack of scholastic ability, for his head was probably full of questions and theories that most schools could not accommodate! Joseff's innate interests and quicksilver mind led to a career in advertising and commercial art. But not before he served an apprenticeship in an art foundry - an important learning experience for his later endeavors. Sensing, however, that his talents were probably more saleable in the glamourous aura of Hollywood, rather than the dreary Midwestern atmosphere of the Depression, Joseff made his way to California from Chicago. Here others were pursuing a similar dream, also hoping to escape the harsh realities of life around them. But they were mainly aspiring actors and actresses. Joseff's path became one of jewels - and ideas!

Through much of this time, however, "He felt...that he was oil in the ink of art; his head was full of Cellini ideas."[2] Surprisingly - or perhaps not so surprisingly if one believes in the existence of deja vu, it was a 1934 movie on the life of Cellini that launched Joseff on the career for which he was to become a legend. This picture was, of course, set in the 1500s, and Constance Bennett, as the Duchess of Florence, was the female star. Whether Joseff enjoyed the movie or not is a moot point, for he was absorbed in the lack of synchronicity between the costumes and sets, and most especially the jewelry worn by the female members of the cast - which was 20th century in design! As Joseff himself described it in a February 1948 article he wrote for *Movie Show* magazine,

> Constance Bennett, incidentally, is really the cause of my starting a jewelry business in Hollywood, although I don't believe she knows it. Some years ago I happened to see a costly production called *The Affairs of Cellini*. In it, Miss Bennett was beautifully gowned in authentic period costumes...and wore a necklace as modern as her personal wardrobe. Up to that time jewelry was only a hobby of mine. But I saw that the studios might use authenticity in jewelry as well as in clothes and settings.

[2] *Photoplay*, February 1943.

61

It took a year and a half to convince them that jewelry was important in the portrayal of a role...that an ingenue shouldn't wear the same kind of jewelry as a dowager. It took all that time to make them realize that the collection of paste pieces they pulled apart and glued together often had no more connection with a period than if they showed an automobile in a picture of the year 1790.

The story goes that when this "conglomeration" of totally inappropriate jewelry assaulted Joseff's eyes in *The Affairs of Cellini*, he told Walter Plunkett, a Hollywood costume designer, that the whole thing looked ridiculous. Plunkett responded, "If you're so smart let's see what you can do." And so, because jewelry portrayed in the silver screen's interpretation of sixteenth-century Italy was four hundred years ahead of its time, Eugene Joseff was inspired to almost single-handedly change the aura of what most audiences took for granted in the re-creation of history - and make believe. And to our great and lasting benefit, movies would never be the same again!

Nothing of substance is as easy as it might appear, however. And little of true meaning is accomplished without roadblocks - and what many might view as insurmountable obstacles. Eugene Joseff's year-and-a-half crusade to bring believability in accessory design to the silver screen was no exception. For when he submitted his intricate designs to jewelers and manufacturers he was told, beautiful and unusual though they were, they would be impossible to produce. Undaunted, Joseff did his own research and made his own tools. When he became fascinated with a particular piece of jewelry, he proceeded to take it apart - and then reassemble it. At first he found himself completing jewelry projects for studios that had already been turned down by manufacturers who deemed their requirements too difficult.

Eventually, with determination to shore up his abundant talents, the name Joseff became legendary on the Hollywood scene, a legend that remains even more awe-inspiring today. Undoubtedly, as is the case with so many great artists in other fields, much of what he produced for these films was probably taken for granted at the time. He was so unbelievably prolific that he made it look easy - the sure sign of a consummate artist! But today these masterpieces can be viewed from a more objective standpoint than did the movie moguls of bygone days - or the rest of us when we paid those dimes and quarters to be transported into fantasy worlds we never dreamed existed. It is claimed that 90 percent of Hollywood movies during that era contained scenes featuring Joseff jewelry. Surely no further proof of Joseff's prolific talents is necessary.

Eugene Joseff brought to his craft a superior knowledge of jewelry making along with great innovation of thought and design, and it was undoubtedly this melding of talents that makes his jewelry so unique. It was, at the very least, a threefold process. He meticulously researched the period being portrayed, created a design concept, and then *recreated* an era from both fact and his artistically tuned imagination. Historian, master jewelry designer, and believer in the ultimate reality of fantasy - it was a potent combination.

By a strange quirk of fate, the bright lights of the movie cameras were a major reason Joseff pieces are frequently muted rather than gleaming with bright finishes. However, there is little doubt that Joseff fully recognized the added beauty these finishes would achieve in the overall image of his designs, especially their softening effect when contrasted to the glittering stones around them. For whatever reason, the result is one element - and a highly individualized one, at that - in the creation of a look that is distinctly Joseff. From cupids, to fanciful animals, to ornate

A faux tortoise handbag by Wilardy seems the perfect accessory for this dramatic parure, consisting of a necklace and earrings by Joseff, and featuring scarabs in multi shades of brown, $1200-1500.

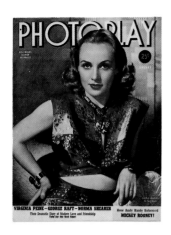

Rear: Four pair of earrings, all uniquely Joseff. Left to right: drop earrings feature diamond-shaped centers with the sheen of black onyx, $175-250; elaborate designs are featured on large Egyptian-influence earrings with three hinged drops, $175-250; "amethyst" stones swing from the center of these engraved circles, $150-200; dainty dangle earrings are accented with pearls, $125-175. Front: Large raised black stones encompass the centers of huge, double-tiered discs (2¾" x 3") in these exceptionally dramatic Joseff earrings, $250-325; 2¾" diameter dome is the setting for the astrological Scorpion, one of a series of twelve brooches created by Joseff, each featuring a sign of the Zodiac, $225-300.

Carole Lombard wears Joseff pear necklace on cover and in inside spread of January 1940 *Photoplay* magazine.

pieces with huge stones and burnished leaves, to masks of fairy-tale splendor, to daggers and swords encrusted with gems, it is unmistakable.

During this period a special line of jewelry apart from that designed specifically for motion pictures was also marketed in major department stores throughout the United States. Immediately successful, American women obviously loved what Joseff created for them, and they flocked to the special promotions that became part of the Joseff mystique. For instance, in 1938 Bullock's department store in Los Angeles staged a promotion of Joseff jewelry featuring a daily promenade in the tea room, and color newspaper advertisements of the latest Joseff designs - surely one of the first uses of color in what was heretofore a staid black-and-white format! In another marketing innovation, the charming and personable Joseff also made frequent appearances across the United States, giving personal attention to the *Jewellery by Joseff* choices of his enthusiastic audiences.

Although Eugene Joseff tragically lost his life in a plane crash in 1948, his wife Joan Castle Joseff carried on the business she had helped him build. This young woman, a recent graduate of UCLA, had entered Eugene Joseff's offices in 1938 in search of a job. "I wanted to go to graduate school, but I needed to earn money first. Well, I fell in love with Joseff the day I met him, and never did go back to school,"[3] says Joan Castle Joseff these many years later.

When tragedy struck in 1948, Joan Joseff was left with the responsibility of either continuing with the Joseff enterprises, or disbanding what both she and her husband had worked so hard to achieve. It was surely an exercise in courage and love, for Mrs. Joseff vowed to go forward with the business her husband had so arduously built.

"Our son was 11 months old. It was left to me to continue. I had to keep going,"[4] Joan Joseff said. And keep going she did. In addition to proceeding with the design and manufacture of jewelry for motion pictures - an awesome undertaking in itself - jewelry by Joseff also continued to be sold in exclusive department stores and boutiques. Mrs. Joseff oversaw this operation as well.

Joan Castle Joseff is full of wonderful anecdotes about her husband's designs. Reminiscing about *The Prisoner of Zenda* she recalls, "My husband made a magnificent crown for Ronald Coleman in that movie. Later when I traveled around the country with some of our movie pieces, I always included that crown. Over the years, people from five real countries came up to me and identified it as the crown of their homeland."[5] Among the vast numbers of movies featuring Joseff's talents were such classics as *Algiers, The Rains Came, Humoresque, Forever Amber,* and the supreme epic of them all *Gone with the Wind!* Not all the jewelry supplied for these films was "costume," however. Many pieces were actually rendered in gold and silver with precious gems. Interestingly, none were ever sold to the studios - instead they were always *rented*. With tales of vanishing film and other lost treasures abounding in today's movie industry, we should all be grateful for that!

Thankfully, these jeweled masterpieces are now part of a three-million piece inventory that is solely controlled by Joan Castle Joseff. It has been made available to the general public only in small quantities, and then usually for the benefit of charitable organizations. For this reason the Joseff designs admired and collected by the public today are most likely those that were, for a relatively short period of time, produced specifically for sale in retail outlets. Although these pieces are wonderfully unique and collectible, exhibiting all of the qualities for which Joseff was

[3] *Almanac,* November/December 1988, p. 28.
[4] *Ibid.,* p. 50.
[5] *Ibid.*

A 2½" wide Joseff cuff bracelet with matching earrings show-case all the exquisite detail for which Joseff was famous—burnished filigree layers offset the pearl and rhinestone accents to create a magnificent setting for whimsical, dangling cupids, $600-800.

The special qualities of Joseff are quite evident in these detailed pieces, each with their own unique ambience. Clockwise: Gigantic 6" x 5" brooch pendant with layered leaves and sapphire blue accents has the appearance of a medieval breast plate, a very dramatic accessory for even a simple dress or sweater, $650-800; intricately detailed 4" x 3¼" brooch with clear pink center accented by four large rhinestones is a symphony of design excellence, $600-700; of the same genre, this brooch also has burnished leaves, punctuated by a brilliant blue stone, a most versatile piece (see hat, p. 11), $375-500; 11" Napoleonic cartouche makes a bold fashion statement on a coat or jacket—or even at the neck of a blouse, $275-375.

With a heart full of gratitude for his many kindnesses to Joseff — Joan Crawford

When Joan Crawford purchased this delightful Joseff necklace, she ran from the showroom with all the bells tinkling... and in the excitement left her mink coat behind! From Joseff archives, courtesy of Joan Castle Joseff.

Clusters of dual-sided seashells dangle from these Joseff earrings, $125-175. 3" Joseff brooch features a tiny angel swinging from this romantic "heart within a heart" design, $225-300.

The unusual combination of an antique finish with a stylized floral design accentuates the bold beauty of this imposing yet graceful Joseff brooch. $200-275

Joan Castle Joseff oversees a dazzling collection of the many crowns of Joseff, circa 1950s.

famous, most of us will never have the privilege of holding in our hands the breathtaking designs that filled the silver screen in darkened theatres during Hollywood's heyday. Nor will we see their like again.

Discounting the fact that the molds cannot be duplicated, to manufacture such pieces today would be prohibitive for many other reasons - not the least of which is the undeniable fact that only Joseff, and the loyal team that carried his dream forward, could create them!

Since 1969, the company has been headed by Karl Eisenberg, grandson of Jonas Eisenberg and Samuel Eisenberg's son, at their Chicago headquarters. His dedication to upholding the stringent Eisenberg traditions remains of utmost importance today and is apparent in each and every piece of new Eisenberg jewelry - just as it was when Jonas Eisenberg fastened that first brooch to the neck of an Eisenberg dress so many years ago!

Six early Eisenberg sterling pieces present a regal display: clockwise, large 2¾" x 2" brooch with ¾" clear stones and interwoven spokes, marked Eisenberg, $750-1000; 2¾" x 2" Deco-style fur clip with subtle insect design and large center stone, marked Eisenberg Original, $700-900; giant 4" x 2" fur clip with magnificent double stones and elaborate leaves marked Eisenberg Original, $800-1100; 3" x 2" floral fur clip of clustered stones and elaborate drops and tendrils, marked Eisenberg Original, $600-800; 2½" x 2½" Deco brooch with spokes of baguettes converging on a large center crystal, with large scrolled E, $700-900; center, rare 3" fur clip of red graduated stones, also with scrolled E, $1200-1500.

Enlargement of red clip above.

This Eisenberg ad appeared in *Harper's Bazaar*, December 1941. Geared to the mode of a sparkling and festive holiday season, how ironic that only a few days after this issue reached the newsstands the United States was plunged into World War II. It is interesting to note that although there was a preponderance of advertisements for "fine jewelry," this was only one of two costume jewelry ads (the other was quite small) appearing in the entire magazine.

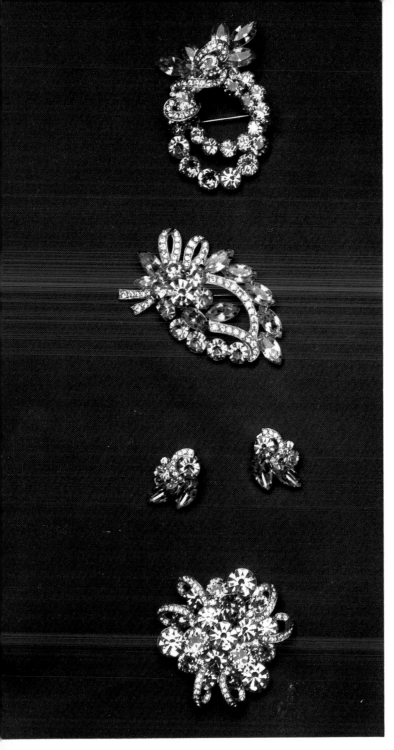

This 3" x 2½" base metal Eisenberg dress clip with huge green cabachons dates from the 1930s and is marked Eisenberg Original, $500-700.

Pastel stones accentuate these intricate Eisenberg designs. Top to bottom: layered brooch of pink and lavender, measuring 2¾" x 1¾", $200-300; dual shades of green are entwined in a pave bow on this 3 brooch with matching earrings, $400-500; brilliant stones, in shades of pink topped with rhinestone accents, form three intricate layers on this 2¼" brooch, $200-300. All marked Eisenberg.

These Eisenberg pieces offer a sharp contrast in size and type, yet all exhibit the workmanship for which Eisenberg is renowned. The pink and red 2¾" clip consists of four overlapping layers, creating an unexpected, yet quite attractive color combination, in a highly stylized piece, with early Eisenberg marking, $450-600. The ring at top right will fool any eye with its faux emerald and diamond look, $75-125. At bottom is a massive 3¾" base metal fur clip marked Eisenberg Original, $600-800.

Unique necklace separates to form one brooch, a single necklace without the "brooch" accent, or two bracelets (see right), $1200-1500; double row bracelet of deep "emerald" stones in graduated shapes is capped with pavé swirls, $250-325; elaborate clear rhinestone and crystal necklace with large, teardrop stones, $350-450. All marked Eisenberg.

Shades of lavender and amethyst highlight these elegant pieces, all marked Eisenberg. At left are large earrings with clear Swarovski stones, $100-125; in center is parure of deep faux amethyst baguettes and rhinestones, $375-450; at right are dainty earrings of pale lavender and clear crystals, $125-150.

Necklace of alternating grey and amber stones, with swirls of pavé rhinestones, marked Eisenberg, is accented by 1¼" earrings of similar coloring, marked Eisenberg Ice. Necklace, $300-400; Earrings, $100-125.

Ever-popular shades of blue dominate these Eisenberg pieces. Clockwise, a 2¼" brooch of layered deep and pale blue stones of varying size, marked Eisenberg, $175-225; pale blue and clear stones form the stems of this delicate brooch, marked Eisenberg Ice, $125-150; elegant necklace of large faux sapphires with accents of pavé rhinestones, marked Eisenberg, $250-350; bracelet of pale blue stones topped with clear rhinestones, marked Eisenberg, $225-275.

Hobé

Before 1868

1868

1883-1902

1903-1917

1918-1932

1933-1957

1958-——

JEWELS OF LEGENDARY SPLENDOR

Hobé et Cie personifies family. That is the overriding message one received upon entering the cozy, working office of Robert Hobé nearly a decade ago. For on a shelf lining one wall are photographs of several generations of Hobés - fathers, sons, and daughters. It's a heartwarming sight, and it sets the tone for the Hobé story that started in Paris in 1887.

Robert Hobé's grandfather, Jacques Hobé, believed that costume jewelry could be manufactured in much the same manner as fine jewelry without sacrificing quality, and that the pleasure of wearing such pieces needn't be confined to the upper echelon of French society. With new manufacturing techniques, he turned his belief into a viable concept, one that his son, William, brought to New York some years later.

A master craftsman in his own right, William Hobé quickly established an outstanding reputation in the United States, founded on the same principles his father had adhered to in Europe. His talents were immediately recognized, and the dazzling results of these unique abilities were soon in demand by a widely divergent audience, including Hollywood stars and producers for whom he created jewelry and costume designs.

In writing about William Hobé, a *Mayfair Magazine* article of many years ago stated, "A connoisseur of antique jewelry, Hobé interprets historical designs into modern settings, foregoing none of the original artistry, no matter the price." Indeed, William Hobé felt that jewelry and costumes were irrevocably intertwined, and he meticulously studied period design, becoming an authority on historical costuming and authentic settings. His expertise came to the attention of Hollywood moguls, and in the ensuing years he created set designs for many epic motion pictures.

Designing jewelry to emulate these periods was a natural outgrowth of this hobby - for his interest in historical settings was initially just that - and the result was a complex intricacy of designs with the look of rare museum pieces.

William W. Hobé

Robert Hobé

Donald Hobé

Each was handmade, frequently involving hundreds of separate parts. It seems a natural transition that Hobé jewelry soon became known as the "Jewels of Legendary Splendor," for not only were they a reflection of the historical legends that were such an important part of William Hobé's life- they were also the epitome of splendor!

Patent design by William W. Hobé. January, 1942. Courtesy Hobé archives.

Over their many years of achievement, Hobé always used semi-precious stones and specially processed gold finishes to magnificent advantage. Some pieces featured large strands of wound and woven gold. Others showcased hematite, pyrite, malachite, jasper, and jade, along with exquisite colored stones in shades of amethyst, topaz, and emerald.

The association of the Hobé name and jewelry continues through the generations. For many years, William's sons, Robert and Donald, proudly carried on the "jewelry dynasty." Bob and Don Hobé are now retired. But not to worry- Bob's son Jim, a talented artisian in his own right, continues to create new designs at his Rhode Island facility.

Hobé at its finest! The much sought-after Hobé bow, in sterling with accent stones of green and amber, 3". $400-600. Hand-crafted 1¾" wide bracelet is a masterpiece of detail and work-manship, with raised flowers, bows, and leaves, $1200+, and cost prohibitive to produce today.

A 4" x 2½ " sterling Hobé brooch marked 14K G.F. Three shades of sterling add yet another facet to this outstanding design grouping, $450-600.

Patent design by William W. Hobé, January, 1942. Courtesy Hobé archives.

Three sterling brooches by Hobé, all with combinations of gold over sterling, with plain sterling stalks, are marked 1/20 14K over sterling, Design Pat. Top two have intricate designs of bows, ribbons and raised flowers. Top brooch is 3¼", $250-350; middle one is 4½", $250-350. Bottom brooch is 5" long and 2¼" wide, $1000+. A truly spectacular piece, with ribboned bow and large pastel stones.

Hobé brooch from group at left shows beauty of design in greater detail.

Three pair of Hobé earrings (green lily pads, $65-85; Deco-style with aurora stones, $50-75; and faux watermelon tourmalines, $100-125) form a backdrop for the delicately layered chrysanthemum brooch, $75-125; Victorian style filigree bracelet with red stones, $175-250; and rolled bar brooch of pave rhinestones with pearl accents, $65-85.

Necklace designed and copyrighted in 1957 by William W. Hobé made with non-precious metal, miniature cameo, and various shaped stones. Courtesy Hobé archives.

Pendant necklace designed and copyrighted in 1957 by William W. Hobé made with snake and link chain, colored stones and pearl. Courtesy Hobé archives.

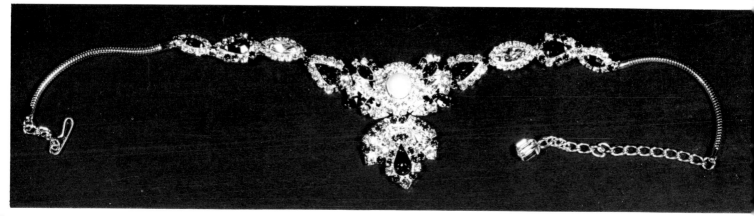

Newest creations in fashion jewelry by Hobé—in the fashion of the Gay Nineties; entirely hand made with simulated stones, meticulously cut as real gems.

Hobé
JEWELS
10 EAST 49 STREET, N.Y.C.
Beverly Hills • Paris • Chicago

Advertisement circa 1957.

Chain rope bracelet designed and copyrighted in 1957 by William W. Hobé, made with non-precious metal, large center stone and surrounding stones of varied shapes. Courtesy Hobé archives.

82

Rare and unique, this Hobé five-piece set, features an 8" hand-bag of lustrous brown velvet with 5½" x 3½" multi-jeweled accent, and an elaborate matching necklace. Combs are 3" wide, brooch is 2¼". Tagged "Jewels of Legendary Splendor," $5000+.

An imaginative design indicative of the era, this purse, with a miniature ivory scimitar that detaches, is from the Hobé private collection and dates to the 1940s, $2000+.

A Hobé necklace with sparkling pendant drop of lavender and purple stones, $150-200; flanked by opulent purple and pearl earrings with 1" center stone, $65-85; and unusual pink and white striated earrings rimmed in blue, $65-85. The 1½" floral brooch has frosted peach and white stones surrounding a blue center, $75-100.

This 45" rope of varicolored beads in unusual finishes and shapes, with matching earrings, is a stunning example of the versatility of Hobé designs, $175-225. At left is an enamel bird brooch, which can also be worn as a pendant, accented with a large jade green center stone, $85-125. On right is a delicate gold butterfly, $75-100. All marked Hobé.

Designs of more recent vintage, all exhibiting beauty and strength of design. Courtesy of Hobé archives.

In the early 1980s, while still involved with his father's New York operation, Jim elaborated on the idea of jeweled drops and other decorative adornments being attached to a simple strand of pearls by designing a removable pearl enhancer. This concept, with many variations, swept through the industry-and into the jewelry cases of women everywhere. Although pearls have always been an elegant and never-out-of-style fashion mainstay, renewed interest has made the enhancer an even more popular item today, and it has now become a jewelry "staple." A later Hobé design further expanded on the versatility of pearls with an ingenious clasp that cleverly converted two strands of pearls into one long and glorious rope!

Jacques Hobé would have been proud of these innovative additions to the faux pearls he created with his own formula many years before. Imported from Majorca-and trademarked under names like Obi and Madonna-the glass base was covered with many coatings of Hobé's secret process, creating a nacreous luster that was guaranteed against defects and discoloration.

Utilizing charming, 20-year-old enamel foo dogs formerly used in a 1960s Hobé design, Jim Hobé also fashioned a striking necklace featuring large, full-dimensional Oriental canines. The result was a contemporary and eclectic look, with a delightful touch of the past to meld it all together.

But it is not just the beauty of their jewelry that commands our respect. It's also the beauty of a family that wholeheartedly believed in maintaining the integrity of what they did so well. That, in essence, is the special aura of Hobé-a sense of the present that never loses sight of the past, and its illustrious origins in Paris those many years ago.

This Hobé parure has everything! The necklace features a variety of stones in subtle colorations, with an unusual raised center section that adds rigidity and holds the intersecting rows in place. The earrings are designed to complement the focal point of the necklace. $450-650

Boucher

The jewelry world has had its share of giants in the field of design, but only a few can be ranked in the very top echelon of this distinguished group. One of these is surely Marcel Boucher, who is held in the highest esteem by former colleagues and competitors alike.

Boucher's story is one of determination and risk-taking. Journeying to the United States from his French homeland in 1925, his prowess in fine jewelry design landed him the position of a designer for Cartier shortly thereafter, a most auspicious beginning!

Eager to explore new avenues, he later expanded his repertoire to the field of fashion by creating shoe buckles and similar accessories for several prominent manufacturers of the era. It was the combination of these two variations on the same basic talent - fine jewelry design and fashion accessorizing - that prompted Boucher to start his own business.

His independent venture into the costume jewelry industry was prophetic of the success he was destined to achieve, for almost immediately he gained the favor of an exclusive Fifth Avenue department store, supplying them with a fashion jewelry grouping designed around an "exotic birds" theme. Utilizing complex enameling techniques and brilliant stones, these multidimensional pieces were an instant sensation, and an exciting alternative to much of the "flat" jewelry that had preceded it. Boucher's training as a fine jewelry designer enabled him to translate these applications into fine *costume* jewelry with a three-dimensional look.

Because of the difficulty in obtaining white metals during World War II, Boucher initiated another operation in Mexico in the early 1940s, and for a time created silver jewelry under the name of Parisianna.

In 1949 Sandra Raymonde Semensohn, who was also from France and had previously designed for Harry Winston, joined Marcel Boucher as a designer. It was a propitious collaboration, both from a business and personal standpoint, for Sandra not only contributed her considerable talents to the Boucher line, she also later became Marcel's wife!

Sandra Boucher continued to design costume pieces and watches for Boucher until 1958, when she left the firm to become chief designer for Tiffany, returning to the Boucher fold in 1960.

Charming! Two bees cavort on a honeycomb in this imaginative and delightful brooch by Boucher, $175-250.
From "The Art of Fashion Accessories" by Ball and Torem.
Photograph by Dorothy Torem.

Marcel Boucher

Sandra Boucher

The success of the collaboration of these jewelry mavens - both of whom had started their careers in the execution of "fine" jewelry - is evidenced by their ability to convert those finite skills to the costume trade. For each design bearing the Boucher mark exhibits the highly coveted qualities one would expect in exclusive jewelry rendered in gold and precious gems. Boucher also added a system of numbering designs, like that frequently used on "jewelry store" pieces. It's an effective touch - one that adds elan to an already masterful rendition.

Marcel Boucher died in 1965, but the firm continued to be active under the direction of Sandra Boucher. However, Boucher jewelry ended in 1970 when the business was sold to Davorn Industries, a manufacturer of fashionable lucite watches, where Sandra Boucher continued as chief designer until 1975. Today she designs both jewelry and watches for major high-fashion clients - and also teaches the techniques of fine jewelry design at the Fashion Institute of Technology, as well as in colleges and art schools throughout the United States and abroad.

Marcel and Sandra Boucher were a formidable team of design professionals. Every piece of jewelry with the Boucher name and number bears witness to Marcel Boucher's versatility and splendid talents - and his belief that costume jewelry could be as beautiful and as carefully crafted as its much higher-priced counterparts regally showcased in the windows of exclusive Fifth Avenue jewelry stores. Without question, he succeeded!

Early Marcel Boucher design drawing. Courtesy of Sandra Boucher.

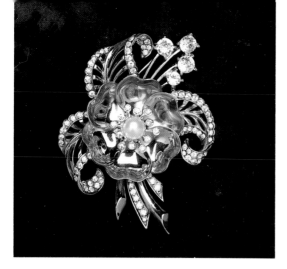

Marchel Boucher's artistry in *fine* jewelry design is apparent in this magnificent example of the costume jeweler's art. This exquisite "night and day" brooch is 3" in diameter and has center petals that open and close at the wearer's discretion. $400-600.

Pineapple with genuine pearl accent, $50-75; large 2½" x 2½" orchid with genuine pearl, $65-85; glass beads of blue and crimson form flowers at top of intertwined stalks, $100-125; 3" flower with pearl center, $65-85.

Earrings of clustered coral beads and pearl centers, $50-60; narcissus brooch with dainty red and pearl center, $50-65. All with florentine and polished finishes, numbered and marked Boucher.

Clockwise: 3" gold fish with spiked scales and green eyes, $200-250; delicate earrings of flowers cupping tiny pastel stones, $55-75; 2½" florentine pineapples are studded with turquoise stones and a pave rhinestone top, $145-175; turquoise stone peeks from top of curved flower with red accents, $125-150; cluster of turquoise beads and rhinestones nestle in this elaborate floral brooch, $125-150. All marked Boucher.

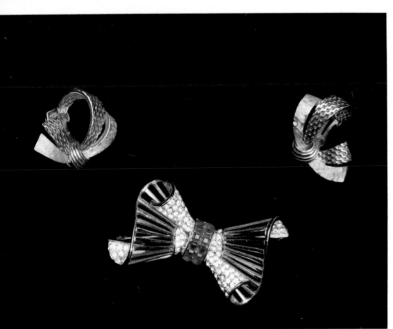

Fluted fan-shaped bow has the decidedly "real" look of Boucher, with its pave accents and faux ruby center, $225-300. The earrings are understated, tasteful swirls, also marked Boucher, $50-75.

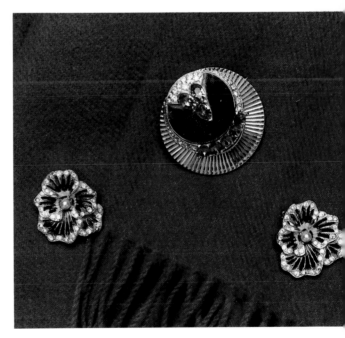

Boucher brooch with "pleated" base has raised center section of opulent faux amethysts surrounded by lavender rhinestones, $175-225. The earrings, also marked Boucher, are dainty pansies with enameled highlights, $65-85.

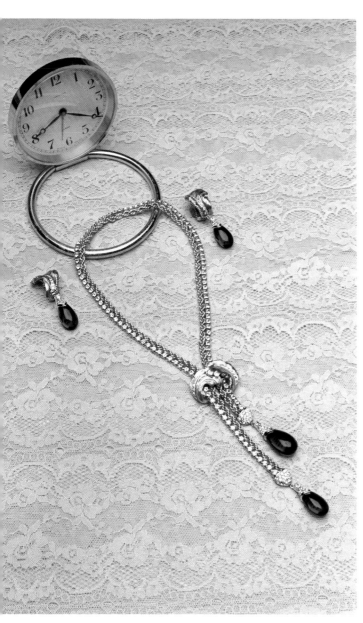

Unusual gold necklace and earrings with "emerald" and rhinestone accents. Center clasp opens to adjust two drops to length desired, $500-700. Marked Boucher.

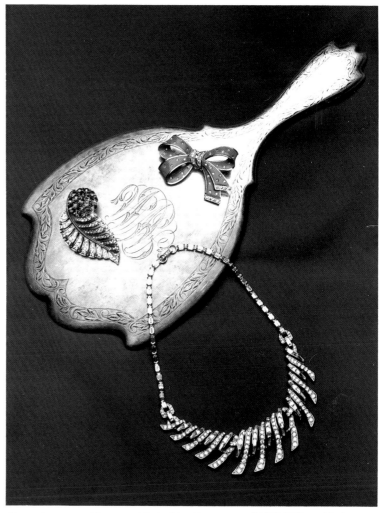

Turquoise enamel bow studded with rhinestones, $150-175; swirled 2½" brooch with faux amethyst cluster, $150-175; both early Boucher, marked MB. Highly detailed, jointed white rhinestone necklace, marked Boucher, $200-275.

The March 1954 issue of *Harper's Bazaar* featured this photo of Maggie McNamara (star of *The Moon Is Blue* with William Holden), wearing a bold Miriam Haskell shoulder necklace of unusual design and coloration. A knockout piece and rare collector's item for anyone lucky enough to own it!

Haskell

To the avid collector the name Miriam Haskell conjures up visions of pearls of all sizes and shapes, twinkling mirrorback stones, fanciful color combinations and muted pearlescent hues, all culminating in jewelry that both excites and enchants. From the boldest to the most delicate, each piece commands our attention and respect. For Miriam Haskell's fertile imagination and love of her craft added a new dimension to fashion jewelry. The results were a unique melding of innovative design and tasteful application into an exquisite piece of art.

Miriam Haskell began her career overseeing a gift shop in New York's McAlpin Hotel. This exposure to the world of merchandising and design stirred her interest in the creation of artistically embellished jewelry, and in 1924 she founded her own company. It was a wise decision, for the refreshing originality of Haskell designs caused an immediate sensation. In ten years' time the business expanded from the confines of a small shop on West 57th Street to Fifth Avenue, where it remained until the late 1960s.

Many of the ideas for jewelry designs from Miriam Haskell's artistic and fertile imagination reached their ultimate completion at the hands of a brilliant artisan, Frank Hess, who continued to create in the Haskell tradition following her retirement in the early 1950s. The privately owned company was then turned over to Haskell's brother, Joseph, and has changed hands several times then.

Having previously been owned by Sanford Moss, in January, 1990 the Haskell operation was purchased by Frank Fialkoff, a leader in the costume jewelry industry whose reputation for excellence is much the same as the woman whose company he now oversees. In a telephone interview, Mr. Fialkoff remarked that when this "jewel" presented itself, he couldn't refuse. "I saw a chance to create fabulous costume jewelry in a company that continued to maintain its taste and integrity. The first time I saw it, I couldn't believe it. Like the great jewelers of the world, we still make every piece by hand and we do it right here in New York. Everywhere there is a sense of reassurance that the 'fine' ways are not gone, that excellence is not compromised."

Although Miriam Haskell died in 1981, costume jewelry enthusiasts can rejoice in Mr. Fialkoff's dedication to maintaining and building upon the imaginative design skills and originality that have become synonymous with the Haskell name.

Today, Haskell pieces continue to dominate the "search for" lists of dealers and collectors dedicated to finding the most appealing examples in vintage costume jewelry

This convertible Haskell necklace is a symphony of design excellence. It can be worn as a long rope with a double floral clasp, or open, as at left. But wait, there's more! When combined into four strands with decorative center clasp, two floral pins remain to either fasten together or wear separately. A truly unique Haskell design, $800-1100+.

Even a classic gold rope of interlocking flexible links reveals the quality of Haskell in its weight and styling, $125-150. The 2½" brooch, with an intricately layered base, has an unusual marbleized forest green center stone, capped with a floral design. The earrings showcase the unique stones to great advantage. Brooch and earrings, $275-350.

Haskell bracelet has three strands of pearls, with starburst clasp of mirrorbacks, $175-250. The 2" brooch encompasses everything one would expect from a Haskell design—overlapping seed pearls, tiny mirrorbacks, delicate burnished leaves, and brilliant center rhinestones, $175-250.

Two Haskell sets recline on a bed of seaglass and sand. Left, luminous coppery beads add an unusual look to this triple-layered 3" brooch with rhinestone edging and matching drop earrings, $275-350. Right, tiny seed pearls and rhinestones stud a honeycomb backing, which encircles a large pearl on both the brooch and earrings, $225-300.

Opposite:
Two Haskell pieces complement sand and shells. The 3¼"
brooch has overlapping burnished leaves with raised accents
of pearls, mirrorbacks, and rhinestones, $200-300. The
pendant, a massive 3¼" diameter piece of faux tortoise,
has center of leaves, beads, and rhinestone rondels, with
scalloped beads crowning each spoke, and elaborate clasp
typical of Haskell, $550-650.

Three striking Haskell pieces of varying colors and designs.
At top is parure in unusual tan and mustard shades with
faux citrine centers, $225-300. At left is a brooch in com-
binations of blue and seed pearls, $200-275; on bottom is
heavy 2" diameter brooch of polished gold with spoked royal
blue stones at tips of each petal, $200-275.

A Haskell symphony in green. The bracelet has strands of
green crystals and pearls, with a huge double clasp featuring a large green cabochon and faux mobe pearl, $275-
350. The necklace has dainty green glass beads with gold
spacers, and a gigantic butterfly clasp that can be worn at
any angle, $300-400.

Sea blue and aqua reflect the delicate beauty of these Haskell pieces. Clockwise: six strand necklace of blue beads and pearls, $200-250; bracelet of aqua beads intertwined with pearls is highlighted by elaborate clasp for which Haskell was renowned, $200-275; brass necklace with delicate filigree pendant rimmed with rhinestones, $150-175; and a four-strand bracelet of blue beads, interspersed with clear spacers, $150-200. Blue earrings, $65-95.

Left top: cuff bracelet with Mobe pearl center, $225-300; Left bottom: burnished wreath brooch is accented by a cluster of fruit, $200-250; Center: double layer of stippled leaves encase coral beads interspersed with tiny rhinestones in this 2¾" brooch, $275-375; necklace with 3" drop and large striated brown stone, $250-350.

Right: necklace of burnished leaves encircles rolls of ceramic coral, $150-200; triple section earrings of tiger's eye and amber stones are accentuated with tiny rhinestones, $75-100.

Opposite:
Top: Haskell earrings (on stand) are part of parure featuring brooch with layers of lavender marbleized stones (below) in a filigree setting, $275-350 set. Brooch is flanked by a floral pearl stickpin with rhinestone center, $135-175; and a dual flower stickpin with large mobe pearls, $150-200.

Bottom: A triple strand necklace of pearls and carved gold beads highlights a 3" brooch of multi-pastel stones, and another dual-sectioned brooch of burnished gold and pearls. Necklace, $350-500; Pastel brooch, $250-350; Pearl brooch, $225-300.

Necklace of multifaceted grey and "citrine" colored beads are intertwined in an elegant Haskell necklace, $175-225. Large, elaborately constructed opera ring, $100-150; stippled stick-pin of same genre, $125-150; and delicate filigree bow rimmed in tiny seed pearls, $100-145. Three strands of milk-glass beads and carved leaves, with a matching clasp, create an unusually feminine bracelet, $145-185.

Pearls, mirrorbacks and tiny rhinestones abound in this grouping of Haskell pieces, each with the highly collectible Haskell "look." Oval earrings, $50-65; Large center earrings, $100-125; Small cluster earrings, $55-75; Brooch and earrings, $200-275; Brooch with pearl, $250-300; Brooch with many pearls, $175-250; Choker, $175-225.

Mazer/Jomaz

The Mazer family, parents of seven sons, emigrated to the United States from Russia in the mid-1920s.

Two of those sons, Joseph and Lincoln, started a shoe buckle business that led to converting low-heeled shoes to high-heeled ones and adding fashionable buckles to the vamps.

However, two other individuals were at least partly responsible for convincing the Mazers to turn their talents to jewelry design and production. One was a gentleman named Orenstein, a stone importer with whom they did business, and who obviously recognized talent and ingenuity when he saw it! The other was Marcel Boucher, then a designer for Cartier, who was responsible for giving us some of the very finest designs and workmanship ever seen in the industry. That, however, is another story.

And so, in addition to providing us with an opportunity to savor the beauty of his own work, we owe Marcel Boucher another debt of gratitude. He encouraged the Mazers to enter the jewelry world - and we are all richer for it. The year was 1927. The costume jewelry industry was in its infancy and the Mazer brothers were at the forefront of the revolution that was just beginning. Through the following decades, the Mazer name held an esteemed place in the industry, and this long-held admiration of their work continues today.

It appears that sometime after World War II the brothers launched into separate operations, explaining the Mazer and Jomaz designations that followed the single Mazer Brothers one. Joseph Mazer's son assumed responsibility for the Jomaz business in the mid-1950s. When he died in the late 1960s, his widow and son continued the operation for a short time, ceasing production of Jomaz jewelry in the early 1970s.

Whether marked Mazer Bros., Mazer, or Jomaz, all jewelry bearing these three names exhibit only the finest in workmanship and design excellence. To hold one in your hand is to see a shining example of what the *golden age* was all about!

This sterling Mazer bow is simple yet elegant. A collector's delight! $200-250.

Opposite page, top:
Blue pearl brooch and matching earrings, marked Jomaz, $150-200.
Large robin's egg blue stone centers this 2" brooch surrounded with elaborate rhinestone design, marked Jomaz, $150-200; frosted white earrings with pearl accents, marked Jomaz, $65-85.
"Amethyst" and rhinestone earrings, marked Jomaz, $65-85; swirled 3" brooch with circle of blue and rhinestones, marked Jomaz, $125-150.

Elaborate 1¼" bracelet, $350-450, and massive 3¼" x 3" brooch, $300-400, reveal detail and stylized look of earlier Mazer pieces, marked Mazer; graceful 3" brooch with large aqua stone, accented by intricate pave rhinestone top and graceful bow, marked Mazer, $225-275.

Below: 3" dogwood brooch with layered flowers, each with red cabochon center surrounded by rhinestones, has gold bee perched on top, marked Jomaz, $300-375; whimsical brooch of cartoon-like cat holding bouquet of flowers, marked Joseph Mazer, $100-125; enameled leopard brooch, marked Jomaz, $175-225; large floral brooch with heavy back and pearl center, marked Jomaz, $100-125; parure of swirled 3" rhinestone rimmed leaf with matching earrings, marked Jomaz, $135-185.

The huge domed turquoise stone in the center of this Jomaz brooch is surrounded by deep garnet cabochons and rhinestones. $150-200

Right: A truly magnificent 6" brooch marked Mazer has four graduated sections with hook at bottom for fastening at desired angle (and to firmly attach to garment), $750-900. Pave and baguette earrings are also marked Mazer, $50-75.

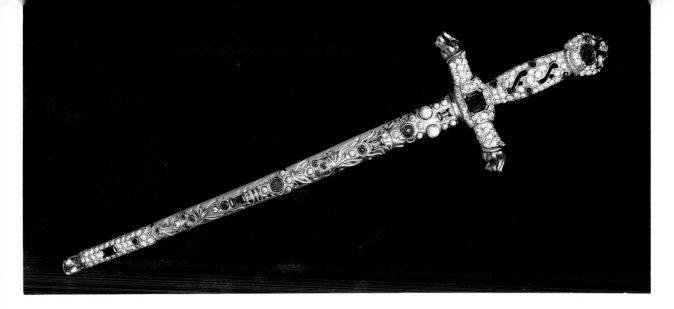

6½" dagger brooch of monumental proportion and design, shows detail of Mazer craftsmanship—including animal heads at each end of crossbar. Marked Mazer, $650-850+.

A starburst design accented by "sapphire and diamond look" stones accentuates this beautiful parure by Mazer in sterling vermeil. The bracelet has three snake chains and side-opening clasp. The center, which is 1½" in diameter, is duplicated in the 2" brooch, and the equally dramatic earrings, $600-750.

Mazer in all its glory! The look of emeralds, diamonds and aquamarine in pieces with the design excellence of fine jewelry. Both the green brooch, flanked by matching earrings, $300-375; and the 3" brooch at left exhibit an uncommonly fluid grace, $375-475.

Two necklace and earrings parures marked Jomaz. On left, pale green, gold-flecked stones, with rigid rhinestone and gold center, and snake chain, $150-200; on right, frosted pale yellow stones are an elegant contrast to the brushed gold and rhinestone accents, $125-175.

Exquisite "emerald and diamond look" 2¼" brooch, marked Jomaz, $300-375; pairs with a 2" wide sterling crown and matching earrings, marked Mazer, $275-350.

A delightful Jomaz owl stands watch over this swirling 2½" brooch and earrings, featuring faux jade centers, and curled leaves of gold and pave rhinestones, also marked Jomaz. Owl, $145-165; Brooch and earrings, $275-350.

Heavy sterling parure marked Mazer has popular Deco look with its large unfoiled ruby-red stones and sparkling rhinestone accents; 3¼" brooch, bracelet, and earrings, $600-700.

The "ruby and diamond" look sparkles in this 5 pc. parure by Jomaz; bracelet, brooch, earrings and ring of exceptional quality. A delightful "fool-the-eye " set, $650-800.

Opposite:
Left: Gold, rigid center, snake chain necklace has emerald green and clear stone accents, marked Mazer Bros, $150-200. Top: Openwork leaf design brooch with matching earrings are in gold with pave edging, marked Jomaz, $125-175. Right: Heavy 2¾" ribbon swirled bow with pave center is a striking example of Mazer workmanship, $250-350. Bottom: twisted gold and dainty pave stones are combined in this ever-popular circle design by Jomaz, $95-125.

Every exquisite piece designed by TRIFARI is a triumph in the art of costume jewelry.

Jewels by TRIFARI

Trifari advertisement which appeared in *Vogue*, December 15, 1944 and *Harper's Bazaar*, January, 1945. Courtesy Trifari archives.

DAY

EVENING

Jewels by TRIFARI
Designs patented

Reprinted from the November, 1946, issue of **HARPER'S BAZAAR**

Trifari advertisement which appeared in *Harper's Bazaar*, November, 1946. Courtesy Trifari archives.

Jewels by TRIFARI

Memo to a smart woman: Circle your choice and slip this page into his pocket.

This Trifari ad appeared in the December 1961 issue of *Life* magazine. Courtesy Trifari archives.

Trifari

Founded in 1918 by Gustavo Trifari, Sr. and Leo F. Krussman as Trifari and Krussman, Trifari is unquestionably one of the "founding fathers" of the costume jewelry industry. Their illustrious history is replete with the rewards of a pioneering spirit and their dedication to the proposition that costume jewelry is indeed a "work of art." To the benefit of women everywhere, Trifari and Krussman accomplished that - and more.

Gustavo Trifari, Sr. was a manufacturer and designer of intricate hair ornaments and bar pins. Krussman, who was employed in the same field, was highly impressed by his competitor. This eventually led to a mutually rewarding merger when these talented individuals decided to combine their respective specialties - Trifari designed, Krussman sold - and establish a new costume jewelry business. Trifari and Krussman was born!

If ever the time was right for a full appreciation of the talents of these two men, it was surely then. The post-World War I years of the 1920s heralded a radical new era. Haircombs became a thing of the past and in their place as *the* fashion accessory was the trend toward *costume jewelry*. In 1925 yet another partner entered the Trifari scenario. His name was Carl Fishel - and thus Trifari and Krussman became Trifari Krussman and Fishel.

Five years later noted European designer Alfred Philippe became an essential member of the Trifari family. Philippe, whose "fine" designs had been sold in Cartier and Van Cleef and Arpels, was at the forefront in the use of brilliant multicolored crystals from Austria to dazzle the senses. Under Philippe's watchful eye, quality and pride of design were never compromised. Each stone was hand-set - just as in fine jewelry - establishing a long held tradition.

In 1938 Trifari became one of the first fashion jewelry companies to advertise nationally, and the slogan of this precedent-setting campaign was "Jewels by Trifari." It was an appropriate choice, for jewels and Trifari have since become as one in the minds - and certainly the eyes - of the buying public. Where else to place these jewels than in a crown? Indeed, the 1941 Trifari crown pin of vermeiled sterling silver replete with brilliant cabochons, rhinestones, and baguettes, created an appealing and much-copied icon in the annals of fashion jewelry design. Trifari stones glittered on the Broadway stage, as well. From the 1930s through the 1960s, they were chosen to design jewelry for many Broadway productions, including "The Great Waltz" and "Roberta."

As with all other private industry, Trifari was subject to the ban on defense-related metals imposed by the government during the years of World War II. Never wishing to compromise quality, Trifari proceeded to produce most of their designs in sterling silver instead of base metals, resulting in a colorful melange, from elegant stylized brooches and fur clips to patriotic jewelry - such as eagles, flags and emblems. Much to their credit, Trifari was responsible for the design and manufacture of England's Royal Air Force emblem, the proceeds of which were contributed to the RAF to assist in Great Britain's war effort.

Other auspicious honors were to follow, not the least of which was being designated, both in 1953 and 1957, to create the inaugural jewels for First Lady Mamie Eisenhower. At the first inaugural, "Mrs. Eisenhower made history and broke tradition twice. She was the first wife of a president to ever wear a pink gown to an Inaugural Ball and the first to wear a set of costume jewelry."[6] Her pink gown was covered with 2000 pink rhinestones, with matching shoes and pink purse, and Trifari presented sketches of designs by Alfred Philippe to complement this historic ensemble. Mrs. Eisenhower chose a three-strand simulated pearl choker with matching bracelet and earrings. This commissioned set was inscribed and presented to Mrs. Eisenhower in a white leather kid case, tooled in gold. In 1957 Mrs. Eisenhower's choice was again pearls, this time a triple strand with rondels of rhinestones and nine pear-shaped drops extending from the bottom.

As reported in a Trifari press release, "Mamie loved pearls and when asked why she chose costume jewelry, she replied, 'The gown called for pearls and I love costume jewelry.'" Former First Lady Barbara Bush was also enamored of the beauty and classic charm of pearls. Since pearls have traditionally symbolized high rank, their choice by Mrs. Eisenhower and Mrs. Bush is surely most appropriate.

Jewels by Trifari continue to be a mainstay of the fashion jewelry world. Over 50 years have passed since Gustavo Trifari, Sr. and Leo Krussman turned dreams and spirit into what was to become a legendary business - a business that has made the Trifari name synonymous with leadership in the world of costume jewelry.

[6] Carter, *Magic Names in Fashion*, p. 199.

This triple-strand pearl and crystal choker was designed exclusively by Trifari for Mamie Eisenhower to wear at General Dwight D. Eisenhower's 1953 inauguration as President of the United States. Courtesy of Cobra and Bellamy, London.

All marked Trifari: Multitone beads of various designs, with an interesting matte look, form three elegant strands in this versatile necklace with matching earrings, $200-300. Two brooches of rhinestone swirls are offset by the always popular bow, this one with a matte silver finish; oval brooch, $50-75, floral brooch, $65-85; Bow, $45-55. Nestled in the silver basket is a rhodium-plated bracelet with dazzling crystal stones, $95-125. Brushed silver finish highlights a bracelet with wide circular links and matching earrings, both reflecting the Art Moderne influence, $65-85.

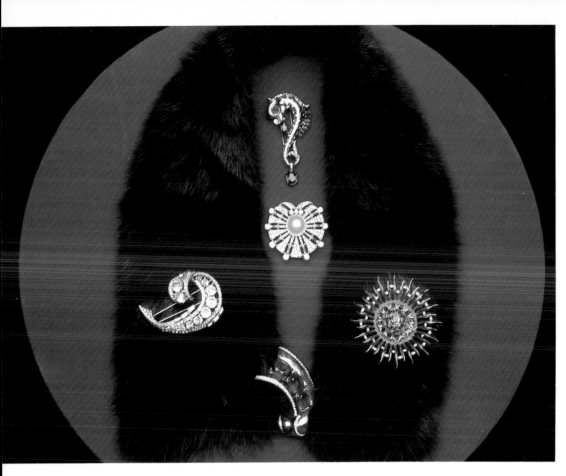

Sterling Trifari fur clips, most with alternate prong for use as a brooch, adorn this fur collar.

Left: heavy base and large brilliant stones form a sterling Deco swirl. $225-300

3" sterling seahorse is studded with red baguettes and a large emerald green drop, $250-400; heart-shaped sterling piece has rhinestone studded spokes and large pearl center, $200-250; another Deco style, this one in vermeil with three exceptionally large red stones, $275-325.

Vermeil 2½" diameter sunburst in shades of lavender and green, $275-325.

Delicate vermeil Trifari brooch has faux blue topaz stones, $150-175; unmarked sterling floral spray, possibly Trifari, $150-200; two sterling Trifari keys, both with crown design, which adds beauty and versatility to a simple "household" item. Vermeil key, $125-175; Sterling rhinestone key, $150-175; vermeil sunburst earrings are same design as lavender fur clip above but have red center stones, $85-100. At bottom is a vermeil pin with eagle and military symbols reflecting a patriotic theme so popular during the years of World War II, $75-125.

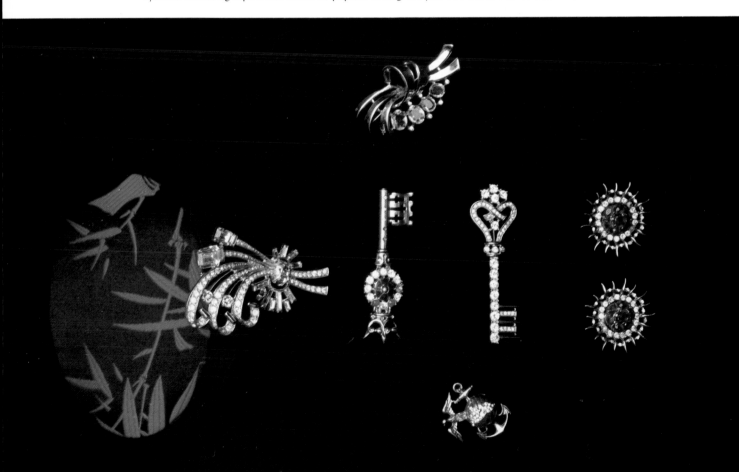

With its elegant horseshoe design, this Trifari brooch has the look of "real" diamonds and emeralds in an array of cuts and styles. $110-135

Below:
Left, top to bottom: Four strands of polished "topaz" stones create these striking earrings, $85-100; bracelet of brilliant, multicolored amber stones, $65-85; combinations of polished and matte finishes combine in this eye catching choker, typical of the Trifari costume look, $65-85.

Center: Matching bracelet and bib necklace, with detailed hinged pieces, beads and bangles, $250-325; dainty bracelet of flowers in muted gold with rhinestone accents, $60-80.

Right, top to bottom: A mix of polished and brushed finishes are combined in this bracelet, $50-75; jointed pieces, again in florentine finish, with pearl accent strips, create an elaborately detailed choker, $65-95.

This elegant Trifari bracelet with aquamarine stones and touches of subtle enameling is designed in the style of its art deco predecessors. $125-165

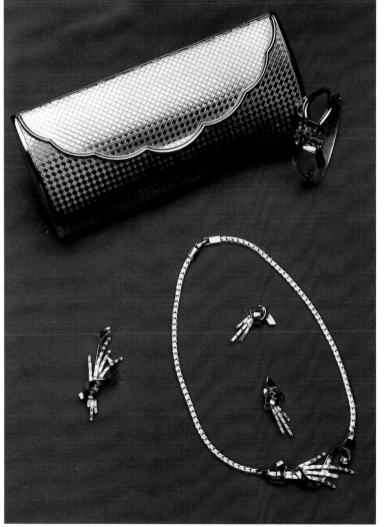

This collection of Trifari brooches presents a broad example of depth of design to be found in jewelry marked "Trifari."
Clockwise: Florentine tendrils highlight this massive yet graceful brooc $65-85; the always popular bird design soars to new heights in piece with polished gold finish, $50-60; faux malachites with rh stone accents are skillfully presented in this simple brooch, reflec the Art Moderne influence, $30-40; starburst brooch of polished g with large rhinestones, $40-55; brilliant rhinestones stud the surf of this captivating brooch with gold center swirl, $75-100; gleam gold provides an interesting contrast to other finishes on this bro with brilliant emerald green center, $65-85; large 3¼" swirl lea understated elegance has heavy polished backing, indicative of m Trifari pieces from this era, $55-65; brushed apple with pave stem large center stones, $50-65. Center: Dainty polished gold brooc accented by rows of rhinestones, $55-65; fabulous 4" leaf brooch v Florentine finish and pearl accents, $75-100; burnished bouquet v exquisite detail is understated, yet classic, $50-65.

An openwork cuff with brilliant red center, $100-145. Four piece parure consisting of necklace with rigid rhinestone center, matching brooch and earrings, $175-225.

Three Trifari necklaces, all with over-tones of the Art Deco period. An elegant trio. Top necklace, $150-200; Center necklace, $200-250; Bottom necklace, $175-225.

This collection of Coro pieces of varying genre gives an overall view of the versatility in the Coro line.

Clockwise: A simple brooch of gleaming gold cherries, $30-40; earrings of brightly colored cabochons and pearls, $40-50, complement a matching 2½" domed brooch, $85-135; pave blue rhinestones twinkle on this delicate gold bud, $55-75; coat-of-arms brooch of burnished gold, $50-70; large 3" flower in enameled reds and brown, with fan of red stones peeking from the top, is typical of early Coro styling, now highly prized by collectors, $165-225; 1940s bracelet of synthetic materials with clusters of rhinestones and pearls, $55-75.

Center: Elaborately jointed necklace in antiqued gold has brilliant stones of soft greens and amber, $200-250; complemented by large floral earrings of glimmering frosted hues, $65-85.

Coro

Founded in the early 1900s by partners named Cohn and Rosenberger, the tradename Coro was a natural outgrowth of the combination of their surnames and, for over half a century, became and almost generic term for reasonably priced costume jewelry.

Indeed, before costume pieces had become a common and desirable accessory for the majority of American women, most of whom were of limited means, Cohn and Rosenberger gambled on the power of their business acumen and a strong belief in what they felt certain would become a fashion trend. The gamble paid off handsomely, for Coro soon became an unparalleled force in the industry - changing the face of "costume" jewelry forever! In fact, the vision of these two gentlemen resulted in a revolution of sorts, for they were almost single-handedly responsible for colored stones and glitter reaching the mass market, and paved the way for others to follow suit.

Their operation was so successful that in the late 1920s Cohn and Rosenberger built their own factory in Providence, Rhode Island, and soon became the leading, and largest, manufacturer of costume jewelry in the United States. In the ensuing years, approximately 50 to 60 percent of all Coro jewelry continued to be produced in Providence, while the remainder was placed in the hands of jobbers.

These pieces, with which Coro flooded the market, caught the fancy - and the pocketbooks - of grassroots America, covering the "five and dimes" that flourished on every main street in America as well as providing more specialized items to other outlets. There was something for everyone, and the female population responded with enthusiasm. Baubles could be bought for a dollar or less, and

Heavenly! A Coro Duette of gilded angels (which can cleverly be worn as two separate pins) shares the limelight with another Duette suitable for the most elegant evening.

suddenly women who had previously been denied the opportunity to enjoy accessorizing with jewelry - at least in any quantity - could now afford to be self-indulgent.

Adolph Katz, who also oversaw the manufacturing facility in Providence, was the major force behind Coro's seemingly endless repertoire of designs. He chose a team of outstanding designers, including Selwyn Young, who later joined Lisner, Gene and Reno Verrecchia, a team of brothers who later founded GemCraft, and Anthony Aquilino. Under Katz's guidance, they and others were responsible for the unusual and often whimsical pieces that collectors are so attracted to today.

During the 1940s, CoroCraft was the strongest link in the Coro chain. However, not to be overlooked was Francois- a small and unfortunately short-lived line that joined the Coro family in 1937, producing many beautiful pieces of top quality. In the 1950s, the high-end CoroCraft line was replaced by Vendome. Soon recognized as a top costume jewelry name in its own right, its chief designer was a woman of exceptional talent, Helen Marion.

Although production of Cohn and Rosenberger's Coro ceased in the 1970s, a look at the history of the costume jewelry industry clearly shows that when these two gentlemen merged the CO with the RO they created more than CORO. They also swept the nation with a gigantic treasure chest of jewelry, and fulfilled their own - and a lot of other - dreams along the way!

This *Harper's Bazaar* Corocraft ad from the March 1954 issue is a delightful look back at a sampling of the bird designs CoroCraft created for the period. It's not surprising they enjoyed popularity then—and continue to delight our senses even today.

With the world still in the throes of World War II, CoroCraft injected a note of whimsy into these somber times with their acrylic "jelly belly" pins, designed to be worn singly or in pairs. Whether creatures of land or sea, they remain a special "find" for the avid collector.

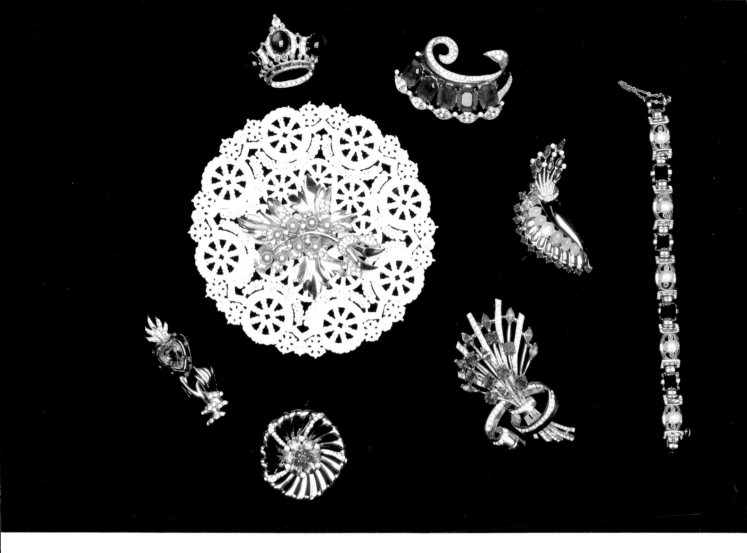

Sterling Coro pieces reflect the eminence of design that marked the influence of this giant during costume jewelry's Golden Age.

Clockwise: Sterling crown is a classic design, $175-225; sterling vermeil swirl fur clip with massive red stones has heavy quality of finer Coro early pieces, $275-350; faux moonstones nestle in the curve of this graceful sterling vermeil brooch, $250-300, bracelet of similar design, $200-250; attention to detail abounds on this massive (3½" x 2") sterling vermeil floral brooch with fan-shaped spokes of colorful rhinestones and a graceful bow, $250-300; circular sterling vermeil brooch has openwork spokes and an aqua/red center, $145-175; hand design, popular yet increasingly rare, is beautifully crafted in this sterling vermeil piece, measuring 2½", $175-225. In center is a vermeil brooch replete with pearls and rhinestones, $225-275. All marked Corocraft.

The design excellence of Francois is evident in this 3" brooch of brushed gold with faux amethysts and movable, overlapping tendrils, $150-200.

A Coro Duette with "everything"! Bottle green enameling, gold flowers with trembling crystal centers, and elaborate rhinestone accents, $275-375.

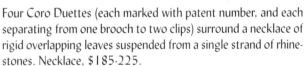

Four Coro Duettes (each marked with patent number, and each separating from one brooch to two clips) surround a necklace of rigid overlapping leaves suspended from a single strand of rhinestones. Necklace, $185-225.

Duettes, clockwise: green gold and rhinestones highlight this simple Art Moderne design, $125-150; red and white enamel decorates this unusual Duette with red tremblers, $275-375; the ever-popular Deco bow in muted pave rhinestones, $125-150; a Duette that says it all—brilliant enameling, an elaborate, heavy design, and tremblers, $275-375.

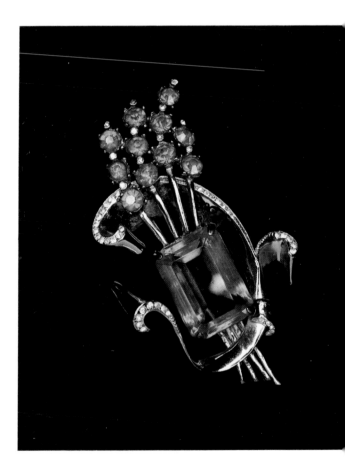

Corocraft at its finest. This 3½" sterling brooch is a swirl of seldom seen rosy-hued vermeil with multiple amber stones and a gigantic faux topaz center, $350-400.

3½" enameled fish with rhinestones and pink cabochons has early Coro style but indistinguishable markings, $185-225; 1940s bracelet of synthetic links embedded with pastel designs, $85-125; unusual Coro Duette in sterling vermeil has enamel birds that can be separated into two dress clips, $275-350; wishbone brooch with raised flowers provides a whimsical glimpse of the past, $50-65; and another Duette has pink moonstones with rhinestone accents, $150-200.

Sterling vermeil flower in pastel enamels with contrasting center stones, marked Sterling Craft by Coro, $95-125; silver and pink earrings with a dainty fruit design, $25-40; graceful flower with aqua stones has look associated with early Coro, $50-65.
Large 3" sterling vermeil bow has brilliant blue stones and center of clustered opalescents, $100-150. Marked Coro Sterling Craft.

Examples of earlier Coro pieces, each with a touch of whimsy—and nostalgia.

Three-dimensional gold angel holds a star engraved with birth month—obviously one of a series, $65-85.

Large bug is studded with colorful pastel stones, $75-110; a variation of the hand brooches so popular during the 1930s and 1940s, $45-65; this "Victorian-look" locket opens to reveal four folding sections for tiny photographs, $65-95.

This "brooch" is a collector's dream. The cartoon-like stick figure with parasol and amusing hat has an equally whimsical dog on a leash, all with touches of enameling, $125-175.

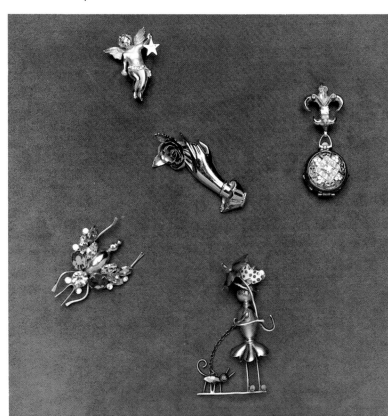

Vendome necklace and earrings are of lacy filigree with brilliant green enamel and rhinestone accents, $350-475.

Vendome

Operated as a subsidiary of Coro, Vendome was a high-quality line that succeeded CoroCraft. Started in the 1950s, but with only modest success, the line was rejuvenated in the 1960s and then achieved the popularity it so richly deserved.

Made with brilliant, high-quality European stones and beads, many Vendome designs are delightfully unique, employing moveable parts and rich enameling. Adolf Katz, the impetus behind the Coro line, also oversaw these Vendome designs. Gene Verri and other fine artisans also contributed their expertise.. However, Helen Marion, Vendome's major designer, was considered by many to be the guiding force behind the ultimate success of the Vendome line.

This showy 5" enameled flower brooch with clustered stones in its domed center is unmarked, but had a Vendome paper tag attached, $150-175.

Florentine gold and rhinestones form a cornucopia with strands of pearls tumbling downward on this brooch by Vendome, $75-100.

Crystals and pearls glow in these necklaces by Vendome. Pearls on the left are interspersed with clear, faceted crystals, $55-65. The necklace on right is a combination of pale yellow, amber, and tan beads, with matching earrings, $100-125.

This 2½" diameter floral brooch with blue center has petals of pale green rhinestones, $65-95; green crystals form the base of this quadruple-layered brooch with gold rimmed green, frosted, and white glass petals with rhinestone tipped pearls in center, $165-200; 4½" black and white enameled floral brooch, with matching earrings, opens and closes by moving slide up and down, revealing stamen inside, $175-250. All marked Vendome.

124

This Vendome necklace is a masterpiece of detail: gold links, clear and iridescent crystals, jet beads, and twisted tassels create an elegant bib, $550-750.

Three brooches show versatility of Vendome line, with each having unique design properties. Top brooch has pearls interspersed with unusual stones of grey and blue, $65-95; center brooch has delicate enameling in shades of soft green with peach accents, $150-175; brooch at bottom is a mass of dangling crystals and pearls, $65-85.

125

Unusual Swiss clock marked Original by Robert is encrusted with pastel stones of all sizes and shape, $250-325; at left is a nest-like brooch of gold with aqua stones, and pendant hook, $145-185; 2½" diameter center brooch of gold leaves with iridescent pale blue center rimmed in blue rhinestones and beads, is shown with complementary earrings, brooch, $175-225, earrings $75-95; large aqua stones set in raised petals give unusual dimensions to this brooch, $65-85. All marked Original by Robert.

Robert

Founded in 1949 by Robert Levy, David Jaffe, and Irving Landsman, the company that later became Robert Originals was originally known as Fashioncraft. When Irving Landsman left the Fashioncraft organization in 1951, Larry Josephs replaced him as the third partner. However, nine years later Josephs departed, and the business was once again in the able hands of two of the original three partners - Robert Levy and David Jaffe. In 1960 the name was changed to Robert Originals, Inc.

This period saw the advent of very dramatic costume jewelry pieces, and Originals by Robert were responsible for many of the most-detailed and elaborate ones. In fact, during the 1960s Robert Originals catered to the theatrical trade, providing memorable pieces for such productions as *Viva Zapata*. Known throughout the industry as a colorful character of spirited imagination and artistic temperament, it was not uncommon for Robert Levy to play the violin while customers browsed through his showroom! A decidedly offbeat touch, that must surely have provided a welcome and amusing diversion for buyers who were racing frenetically from showroom to show-room to make their seasonal choices. Robert's artistry was probably not the only motivation for his musical interludes, for they also exhibited his prowess as a marketing genius.

Although Robert may have been a "character" in the nicest sense of the word, the fact that his magnificent designs were taken seriously in all areas of the trade is evidenced by his being named recipient of many well-deserved honors, including the exclusive Coty Award in 1960.

In 1975 Robert Levy retired and Ellen Jaffe, David Jaffe's daughter, joined the company as designer and president. In 1979 the company name was changed to Ellen Designs for Robert Originals, becoming solely Ellen Designs, Inc. in 1984.

Ellen Jaffe Wagman and her husband, John Wagman, now run this New York-based company, continuing to offer jewelry of quality and imagination. The business started decades before by Robert Levy and David Jaffe is in good hands!

Unusual finishes and enameling form the base for these Original by Robert pieces.

Hinged enamel bangle in shades of blue and purple, $125-150; huge 4½" brooch has an intriguing center stone of shaded burgundy, and multiple strands of gold capped chains, $600-800; 2½" Deco brooch in subtle insect design has accent stones of pale amber and olive green, $250-325.

Four-piece parure is a masterpiece of design and execution. Enameled flowers of rich blue on burnished leaves, each with a rhinestone and pearl center, are interspersed with gold, pearl and rhinestone accents, $450-650.

This Robert bracelet has exceptionally large 1½" clasp, all done in shades of white and cream with overlapping gold leaves, $250-325.

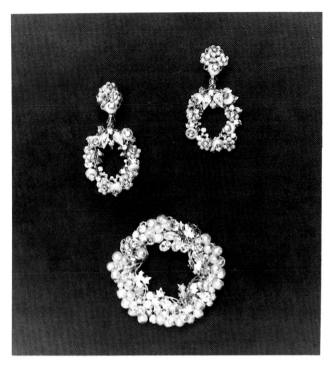

Interwoven pearls and tiny sparkling rhinestones on antiqued silver highlight these pieces by Robert. The brooch, $250-325, looks like a glittering holiday wreath and the earrings, $150-175, are equally festive. Great together or stunning as single pieces.

Frosted pale yellow stones, strands of pearls with matching cream-colored chains, and large, double layered center flowers, create this unusual parure. Brooch is 3", $500-600. Marked Original by Robert.

Detail for which Robert Levy was renowned is evident in these pieces. Clockwise: 3-strand bracelet of alternating pearl and aqua beads, clasp of intertwined matching stones with iridescent center, $125-165. Brooch and earrings of chartreuse and pale blue enamel with rhinestones, $175-225. Pale pink enameled earrings are double layered with rhinestone clusters, $85-125. All marked Original by Robert.

129

Although noted for the craftsmanship of his sophisticated designs, Robert also produced outstanding enamel pieces, usually of colorful floral subjects like the two shown here. $65-85 each.

Brooch and earrings are layered with spiral prongs encasing brilliant rhinestones of varying size. The 2¾" x 2" brooch has a ¾" depth, $250-325; strands of delicate seed pearls are intertwined with a double strand of larger ones, culminating in a magnificent floral front clasp with pearlized finish, $500-750; burnished silver filigree forms the base for this 2½" brooch and matching earrings, both layered in an unusual variety of stones with blue/grey overtones, $250-350. All marked Original by Robert.

Polcini

In 1911 Ralph Polcini, a goldsmith from Italy who immigrated to the United States in 1896, founded a costume jewelry company called Leading Jewelry - an idea adopted by only a few other forward-thinking individuals in a culture that had shown little inclination to move in that direction.

Polcini's intent was to maintain the same standards and methods he had previously applied to the goldsmith trade, and it was that accent on quality by him and other jewelry pioneers that brought about the eventual turnaround in the perception of *costume* jewelry. The many awards Polcini received in the ensuing years, including recognition from his homeland in the Italian version of *Who's Who in America*, is clear-cut evidence of the success he achieved.

Polcini's son, Damon, brought the term "learned at his father's knee" to graphic reality, for that's exactly what he did at the age of five when he began observing and working alongside Ralph Polcini.

Leading Jewelry was renamed Ledo in 1949. When Damon Polcini inherited the company business in 1954, he continued to produce the quality designs for which his father was renowned, and in 1960 the company name was once again changed - this time to Polcini, in honor of its founder.

In the early 1970s a jewelry and accessory designer, Lee Menichetti, discovered some old molds in Polcini's factory and decided to recreate a *new* collection for the company, harkening back to themes from the 1920s. Covering a wide range of diverse subjects like touring cars, golfers in Bobby Jones knickers, and flappers with bobbed hair, most were encrusted with pave rhinestones. A particularly intriguing reproduction from the 1930s featured glittering crystals on black suede figures with cameo heads!

However, many other old Polcini designs, some of which had been sand-casted, were considered too expensive to reproduce. As Damon Polcini explained in a 1971 *Women's Wear Daily* article, "They were all hand-set rhinestones and a setter can only do two or three a day. They would have to be hand set to keep the luster and beauty - I would never paste them."

This dedication to maintaining the high standards set by Ralph Polcini made it particularly unfortunate when companies became the unwitting victims of the upheaval that swept through the costume jewelry industry in the 1970s. Polcini was forced to close their major manufacturing facility and continue production on a very limited scale, leading to the eventual shutdown of operations several years prior to Damon Polcini's death in 1984.

It was then that Polcini's widow, Paula, and their three daughters, Pamela, Christina, and Luane, decided to revive the business and continue the family legacy left them by Ralph and Damon Polcini. A return to the appreciation of fine costume jewelry was on the horizon, and the Polcini's decision to reclaim their position in the business was well timed.

Ralph Polcini

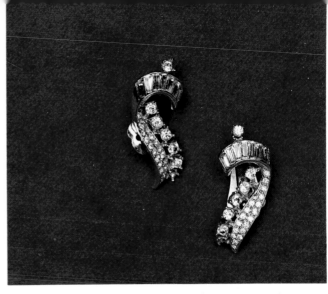

This pair of Ledo earrings in swirls of baguettes and multisized rhinestones are a Polcini creation, $75-100.

Pamela Polcini, as chief designer, employed and elaborated upon the methods used by her father and grandfather, resurrecting and redesigning many of the wonderful pieces that had made Polcini such a respected name in years past.

The jewelry industry is - in somewhat subtle ways - a family unto itself, and many of these long-time craftsmen, along with old and new clients, undoubtedly welcomed the Polcini name back into the fold!

Original Ralph Polcini design, circa 1930. Courtesy of the Polcini family archives.

Ledo ad from the 1940s or early 1950s. Courtesy Polcini archives.

These pieces are courtesy of the Polcini family, from their private collection. Stunning in design and execution, they are a tribute to the talents of Ralph and Damon Polcini. The birds are in a rarely seen double clip, marked Ledo, $350-450. The blue-stoned brooch at top right is in a subtly intriguing snake design, marked Ledo, $200-300. The two bar pins are from the 1920s, during Polcini's early "Leading Jewelry" period, $175-250 ea. The lavender pave rhinestone flower at bottom left is from the 1960s or early 1970s and marked Polcini, $400-600, as is the massive rhinestone piece at the right, $350-400. The glorious center bracelet, marked Ledo, is astounding in design, $500-700.

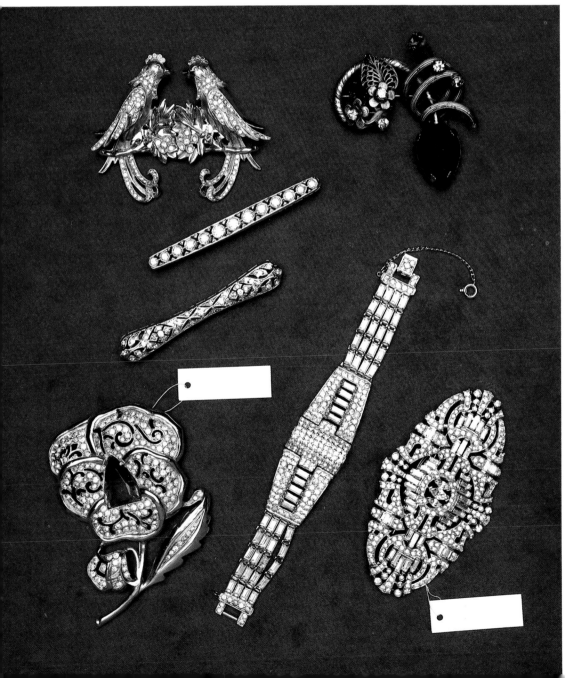

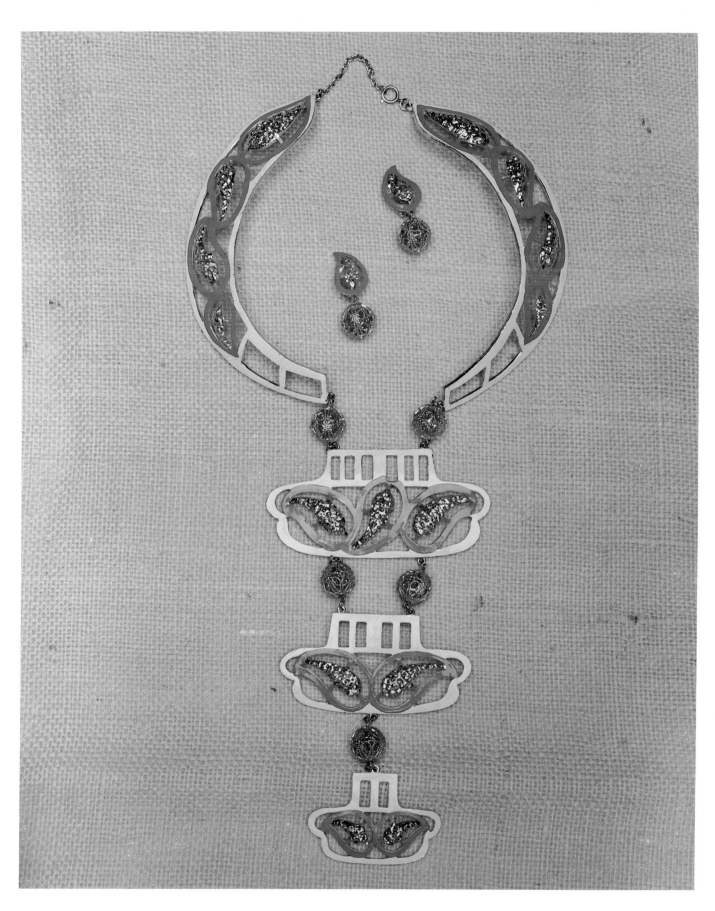

Dramatic Polcini necklace with rigid enameled sections and gold accents, with matching earrings, $325-450.

Ciner

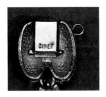

Entering the showroom of Ciner is like a visit to fairyland! Heavy ropes of luminescent pearls, interspersed with magnificent stones and sparkling rondels, cascade in colorful, breathtaking displays. Other pieces of equally elaborate detail fill display shelves and meticulously arranged silver boxes. The quality is unmistakable and awe-inspiring.

It is this uncompromising care that has been the hallmark of the Ciner name since its founding in 1892 by Emanuel Ciner, who at that time manufactured jewelry of only gold and precious gems. However, in 1931 the company's focus shifted to the design and manufacture of costume jewelry, which was then in its infancy. The Ciner name at once signified the very finest in quality jewelry of this relatively new genre, a designation that remains today.

Sold in only the finest stores throughout the world, Ciner jewelry continues to be manufactured in their own factory, which is located in the same building as their showroom. Each step in the meticulous process of producing jewelry of this caliber is done by hand by skilled model makers, casters, polishers, stone-setters, and enamelers. Every pearl and bead is hand-strung and hand-knotted. All stones are hand-set. Each piece has an 18-carat gold plated finish.

Even though the jewelry is so carefully crafted, the Ciner line is vast and diversified. Opulent stones that glisten like real gemstones share the limelight with more classic yet equally lovely designs. As would be expected in jewelry of such fine quality, the prime supplier of stones is Swarovski. The pearls - especially made for Ciner by Japanese artisans - are glass-based beads that have been coated many times with a luminescent finish that gives them the beauty of cultured pearls.

Ciner has come a long way from the gold designs of the early twentieth century, as evidenced by their magnificent chains of pearls, animal clasps, and classic daytime gold, some incorporating delicate pave stones and others in chunky sculptured pieces of both gold and silver.

Although it is not surprising, it bears repeating that the lucky owners of earlier Ciner pieces have found them to be as beautiful now as when they were bought. One look at Ciner jewelry today is convincing testimony that future generations will be equally as pleased.

And so, although change has surely taken place over the last half century and more, Emanuel Ciner would undoubtedly be proud of the fine jewelry that continues to bear his name.

This stunning Ciner clip of bowl-shaped leaves with rows of glittering rhinestones across the top dates from the 1920s or 1930s. A very real look, spanning over half a century, $135-175.

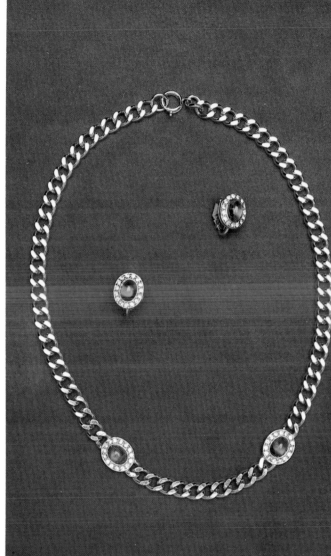

This delicate Ciner set quite effectively mimics the "real thing." After many years, the gold chain retains its perfect finish and the stones have the lustre and clarity of emeralds and diamonds, $175-250.

Four Ciner pieces of 1950-1960 vintage. Top to bottom: brushed gold butterfly brooch with pearl and rhinestone accents, $125-150; sea creature brooch layered with tiny pearls, $100-125; brushed gold bracelet with dainty turquoise stones, $125-175; wide cuff of interlocking white sections, $150-200.

Magnificent! This parure is an outstanding example of finely crafted "costume" jewelry looking as smashing as the "real thing." Courtesy of Ciner Jewelry. Earrings, $300+; Necklace, $1500+; Bracelet, $700+.

Dragons! Eagles! Butterflies! All are marked KJL. Shells form the butterfly's body, with its massive 3½" wing span, $275-350. The double-headed eagle, highlighted with brilliant cabochons and a pavé rhinestone body, is 3" long, $325-450. Rhinestone accents, a green cabochon eye, and even the darting tongue, complement the graceful lines of this 3" dragon, $300-400.

138

$\mathscr{K.\ J.\ Lane}$

A legend in his own time. That's Kenneth Jay Lane. Urbane and witty, Kenneth Lane infuses today's costume jewelry industry with a renewed aura of sophistication and elegance. Each collection offers new challenges, and the fact that designs in his latest collection exhibit the same freshness and originality as his first is a rare attribute - and the signature of a dedicated entrepreneur!

Since its inception in 1963, KJL jewelry has enchanted women from all walks of life. First Ladies as disparate in style as Jackie Kennedy, Nancy Reagan, and Barbara Bush chose Kenneth Jay Lane jewelry to complement and accentuate their own individuality. That jewelry of such differing ambiance could be the work of the same company is a tribute to the integrity of Lane's vision and the interpretation of that vision into a multitude of designs of wide-ranging scope and appeal. For each is uniquely Kenneth Jay Lane, and each is just as uniquely the personal fashion statement of the wearer, such as the much-admired strands of olive-sized pearls that became the fashion trademark of former First Lady Barbara Bush.

Kenneth Lane began his career with a stint in *Vogue's* art department. He also was associated with Delman Shoes and Christian Dior. But it was his ingenuity in placing rhinestones on footwear that motivated him to convert this idea to jewelry design. While doing a collection for Scassi, he developed a technique for pasting flatback rhinestones on jewelry to match the ornaments on the shoes, and thus a new facet of his career was launched. Today Kenneth Jay Lane jewelry continues to dominate the runways of many couture collections.

Lane was at the forefront of designers who saw the revolution in fashion created by the "beautiful people" of several decades ago. As he recalls, "They started dressing up a lot, and costume jewelry was rather dull. I believed it didn't have to be."[7] In fact, Lane saw no reason why fake jewelry couldn't be as beautiful as the real thing. To illustrate the validity of his conviction, dime-store plastic bracelets became objects of beauty and respectability when he covered them with crystals and rhinestones. Thus, a new look in fashion jewelry was born.

At least one guideline of the true artist, whether it be a painting or a beautiful piece of jewelry, is to create by his or her own rules. Kenneth Lane has always adhered to that principle. "I work in less commercial ways than most manufacturers of costume jewelry. They work seasonally, but I do not believe there is a season for jewelry. I like to create jewelry that can be worn any time of the year. I like my jewelry to be classic, something that is collected rather than bought for a season."[8] Lane's maxim has certainly been achieved, for his jewelry is treasured by collectors and aficionados of fine design regardless of the medium, as well as by the vast following of devotees who wear them time and time again, season after season.

[7] From Kenneth Jay Lane archives and personal interview.
[8] *Ibid.*

That these pieces continue to be appreciated and admired is a tribute not only to skill of design but attention to craftsmanship as well. For as in fine jewelry, the designs are cast in wax or by carving or twisting the metals. Lane is especially proud of the stones that he perfected and personally developed with his supplier in Germany. They are strikingly different in color and luminosity. Unfoiled, they look like real rubies, sapphires, and emeralds. Although he uses the brilliant Swarovski crystals from Austria for his clear stones, these colored ones reflect not only their own beauty, but also the continuing innovation and dedication that Kenneth Lane brings to his work.

A trendsetter in many areas of design, Lane's personal preference is for the beauty of Art Deco. Indeed, his reintroduction of that era in his jewelry designs during the 1970s and early 1980s caused a renewed interest in the original Deco pieces, as well as the counterparts so faithfully produced by Kenneth Lane in his own design interpretations. While not particularly fond of abstract or modern jewelry, Lane finds that the Deco period also translates better and is not prohibitive to the "real" look he's achieved in costume jewelry. As with Deco, the Egyptian motifs of the mid 1930s were also reinterpreted in the KJL line, and they, too, have attained a renaissance of interest and new fashion stature.

Lane is proud to point out that the sale of the late Diana Vreeland's jewelry in 1987 was arranged by him, including the introduction he wrote to the catalogue, and that many of the offerings were of his own design. He also created the jewelry for Vreeland's Costume Institute exhibitions at the Metropolitan Museum of Art.

The same meticulous attention he devotes to the design and execution of his jewelry is also evident in Kenneth Lane's personal style - and his numerous awards. Consistently on the International Best Dressed Men's list, he has received the Coty American Fashion Critics Special Award for "Outstanding Contribution to Fashion" in addition to many other industry citations.

Exclusive of the special collection he prepared for Avon, Kenneth Jay Lane jewelry, as well as handbags, watches, belts and hair ornaments, are sold in department and specialty stores throughout the world. Except for the magnificent shop he maintained in New York's Trump Tower and boutiques in London, the other specialty boutiques bearing his name were later operated by Ciro.

Opposite:
This green pear, with pave stem and leaves, is 2¾" long and has a polished green, marbleized finish, $185-250. Marked KJL. The earrings have an exceptional depth of 1", with rims studded with faux lapis, and rhinestones encircling the large faux pearl centers, $125-150. Very outstanding, and marked KJL Laguna (a company noted for their pearls).

This 2" KJL bug had dual appeal. Wear it closed for a more sedate look, or open the wings to reveal a dazzling rhinestone body, $250-300.

Kenneth Jay Lane's jewelry has been worn in most ingenious ways. In fact, at Truman Capote's famed "Black and White Ball" an ornate necklace became a mask when artfully draped over a guest's forehead and eyes.

"The bold and the beautiful." Three necklace and earrings parures are fine examples of the look that has made Kenneth Jay Lane a legend in his own time. Eleven strands of grey pearls are caught in a massive clasp of white enamel with ribbons of gold and rhinestones; matching earrings have large grey mobe pearl centers, $350-450; double strand of large cylindrical pearls has four-petaled rhinestone clasp with large center pearl; earrings match the clasp, $250-350. Acrylic flowers in shades of lavender are rimmed with rhinestones in this very feminine piece; matching earrings complete the flower motif, $300-375. All marked Kenneth Lane.

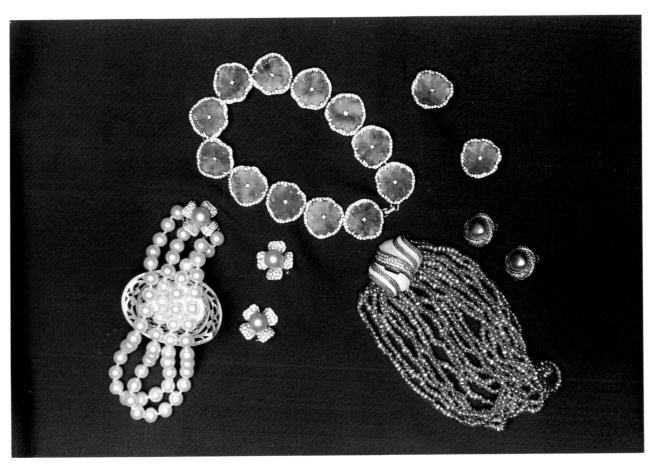

Top: belt of white glass beads and gold accents creates a versatile accessory, $225-275. Marked KJL; bottom: necklace of twisted coral, turquoise and white beads with gold spacers and elaborate clasp, $185-250 marked KJL; heavy cuff of gold with white cabochons and matching earrings, $200-250. Marked KJL.

Opposite:
L. to R.: Known as the "Jackie" necklace, this was copied in various colors and stones, reputedly at Jackie Onassis's request, from a "real" necklace given by Aristotle Onassis to his new wife. Regardless, this parure (with brooch, not shown) is pure dynamite! $2000+. Marked Kenneth Lane. Amulets dangle from this heavy brass pendant with red center stone, marked KJL, $125-175; black synthetic stones gleam like onyx in this necklace and earrings parure with an Art Modern influence, $275-375. Marked Kenneth Lane.

Water and land creatures cavort in this KJL display. At rear is 3" octopus with gold and rhinestone tentacles and moveable "head", $350-450. In front is a ferocious hippopotamus enameled in a rich eggplant shade and sporting a rhinestone collar, $275-350. A captivating lion with gold mane and rhinestone body has the look of "precious" jewelry, $175-225, and the swan floating on a mirrored lake is, in fact, a heavily encrusted pillbox, $125-175. All marked KJL.

This massive cuff bracelet makes a distinctive fashion statement with its heavy gold finish and huge center crystals, each measuring 1" square, $275-350. Marked KJL.

Left: Shades of mauve and lavender are combined in flat and sparkling finishes on this two-strand necklace with frosted floral drop, $300-400. Center, pink stones, pearls, and mirrorbacks unite in a dazzling, multilayered brooch, $150-200. Right, a choker of double strands of faux pearls and mesh bow clasp, which can be worn at front or side, $165-200. All marked De Mario.

De Mario

A freelance jewelry designer prior to World War II, Robert De Mario founded the company bearing his name shortly after the war's end. In business only until the late 1950s, it was a loss for the industry and devotees of fine jewelry design when De Mario decided to end his illustrious career and retired to Palm Beach. Contrary to popular belief, DeMario never designed for Miriam Haskell.

Collectors of this beautiful jewelry, all of which are outstanding examples of "golden age" craftmanship, are surely justified in coveting these carefully executed treasures. Their exquisite beads and delicate workmanship are easily recognized as coming from the talented mind and hands of Robert De Mario.

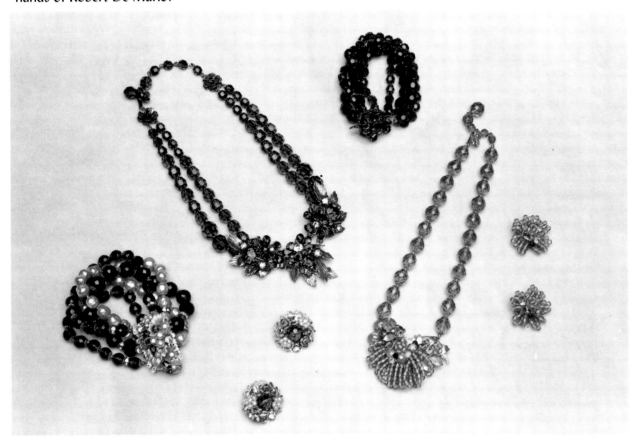

Brilliant green parure consisting of necklace with elaborate three-section floral accents and "pewter" look leaves, and to it's right, bracelet with matching clasp, $375-475; bottom: another multistrand bracelet has massive, elaborately detailed clasp, $185-225.
Right: Dainty, twisted beads with muted burnished shading form this necklace and earring parure, $175-275, flanked on left by pair of green and gold beaded earrings, $45-65.

Pastels abound in this multicolored four-piece De Mario parure of faux pearls and clear, marbleized, and iridescent stones, $325-400.

Necklace of sparkling red crystals and pearls, $125-175, is flanked by another in shades of blue interspersed with gold chains, $150-200, red aurora earrings, $30-50, and bracelet of intertwined orange beads and pearls with elaborate clasp. $145-185. All marked De Mario.

Kramer

Kramer Jewelry Creations was founded in 1943 by Louis Kramer, who was later joined in this newly booming costume jewelry explosion by his two brothers, Morris and Harry. Kramer, with the able assistance of his siblings, not only managed the manufacturing operation but also personally contributed much to the design of these elaborately beautiful pieces. That he also carefully controlled the integrity of the finished product is obvious in each and every piece of Kramer jewelry.

Although some designs were simply marked Kramer, it was fitting that many bore the inscription "Kramer of New York," since all aspects of manufacture were confined to New York City. During the 1950s, the Kramer operation was also responsible for the production of Dior jewelry in the United States, and these exceptionally fine designs were appropriately marked "Dior by Kramer" (see pages 34 and 35).

Kramer jewelry has not been marketed since the late 1970s, but the contribution of the three Kramer brothers to the beauty of the *golden age* remains a lasting one.

2½" floral brooches marked Kramer, both with matching earrings. Brushed violet parure has gold rim, accented by blue pearlescent beads and tiny fuschia stones, $150-200. Five-layered flower in pink and green enamel has rhinestone "trembling" center, $275-350.

Intricately detailed 2" king of hearts brooch, with king in raised relief, $200-275, is flanked by a red enamel leaf brooch, $45-65, a brushed gold leaf brooch and earrings with rhinestone accents, $95-135, and a swirling rhinestone brooch, $125-175. All marked Kramer.

Five piece Kramer parure, consisting of jointed necklace and bracelet, with matching brooch and earrings. All have pale green and white enameled flowers, each flower with a rhinestone center. A masterpiece of design and workmanship, $375-450.

These Kramer parures could adorn the finest garments without arousing suspicion as to their authenticity. Top pieces feature large faux sapphires surrounded by pave rhinestones, $165-225. Brooch at bottom has crystals and rhinestones in a stunning leaf design, $150-200 (parure).

Frosted pastel "ribbon candy" bow, $55-65; center, top to bottom: earrings of acrylic pale blue flowers with aurora borealis centers, $40-50; brooch of pale frosted yellow stones, $50-65; 2¼" brooch has aurora borealis stones on rigid base, with dangling crystals and yellow beads, $75-100; right: 1¼" leaf earrings are mother-of-pearl on a silver base with raised rhinestone accents, $50-65. All marked Kramer.

The intensity of the light plays tricks on this center bracelet, changing the color from lavender to pale blue, $150-200. It is flanked on the left by a brooch and earring set of burnished grey, with aurora blue stones, $135-175, and dangling drop earring of frosted clear, and luminescent stones, $65-85. All marked Kramer.

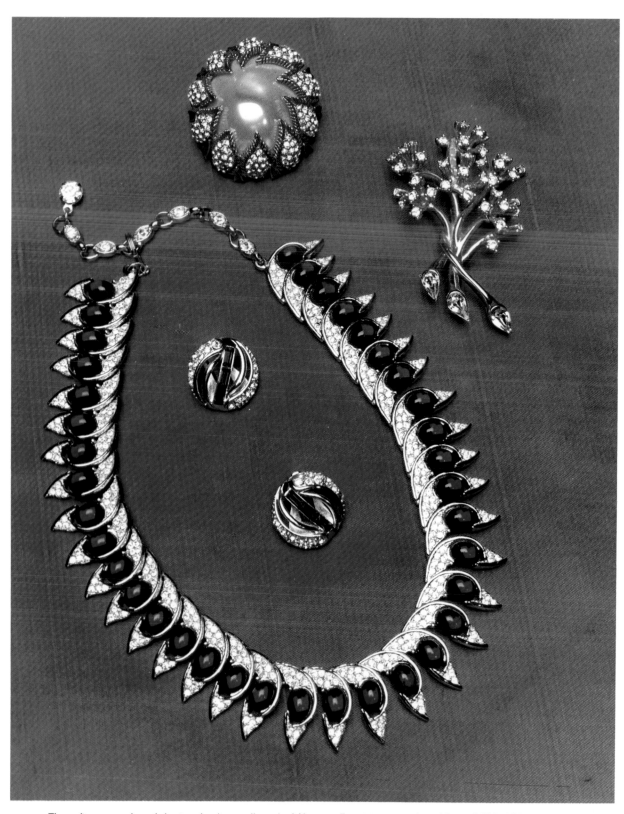

Three fine examples of the jewelers' art, all marked Kramer. Exquisite jointed necklace, $325-425, with matching earrings, $50-60, has delicate pave rhinestones encircling brilliant emerald cabochons; leaves of pave rhinestones and braided gold encapsulate a huge faux mobe pearl in this brooch, $85-135; another brooch has gold branches forming a tree of rhinestone blossoms, $145-185.

Weiss

Founded in 1942 by Albert Weiss, who had formerly worked for Coro, the Weiss company specialized primarily in high-quality rhinestones in white and colors, along with outstanding floral and figural designs like butterflies and insects.

When Albert Weiss retired, the business was turned over to his son, Michael Weiss, and continued to be family operated until closing its doors in the early 1970s. This was a real loss for collectors who still prize the Weiss name, and would surely welcome more Weiss designs to add to the pieces they enjoy now.

Four pieces typical of the "look" of Weiss. 3" trembler of white and green enamel is accented by brilliant blue and green stones, $145-175; two butterflies, one of sparkling faux citrines, $165-225, the other with frosted yellow stones and amber accents, $135-165; the earrings also have stones of yellow and amber, $40-55.

Large fuschia stones are encircled by rows of tiny rhinestones in this showy Weiss brooch and earrings parure, $185-250.

The beauty of rhinestones by Weiss shines through in this grouping of mixed pieces. Clockwise: $75-85; $135-165; $35-45; $65-85; Center: $135-175.

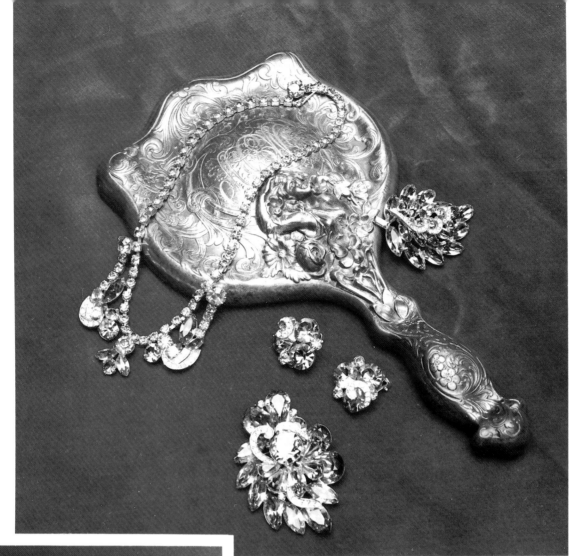

Necklace, brooch and earrings, and single brooch are all fine examples of the grey/rhinestone pieces, appropriately called "black diamonds," for which Weiss was renowned. Necklace, $200-275. Brooch and earrings, $175-225. Single brooch, $95-150.

A hinged cuff of amber stones contrasts with three green brooches of differing designs and stones. All marked Weiss. Bracelet, $85-125. Brooches, top to bottom, $110-140; $75-95; $95-125.

153

Necklace of multi-pastel stones and early slide clasp, $175-225, is flanked by a brooch of woven wire that forms a "nest" of faux jade and pearls, $75-100, and composition earrings of pale pink with rhinestone insets, $40-55. All marked Weiss.

These Weiss pieces are a study in pale blue and rhinestones. The center necklace and earrings, $375-500, have clear, faceted blue stones of exceptional clarity, creating a parure of special beauty and workmanship. Bracelet, $85-125. Brooch, $65-85. Earrings, $50-65.

M. Barclay

McClelland Barclay was a respected artist renowned for his illustrations and magazine covers in the 1930s. Jewelry bearing the McClelland Barclay name was produced during this time as well, but Barclay's many-faceted career was tragically cut short by his death in action during World War II. An eclectic designer, Barclay's name also appears on items like statuary, vases, and aluminum pieces.

Striking in it's Deco beauty, McClelland Barclay's jewelry is unmistakable in its unique style and execution - that is if one is lucky enough to find or own a piece! That these "gems" are the work of a multi-talented artist is clear, each bearing witness to the genius the jewelry industry, and the art world, lost so prematurely.

McClelland Barclay pieces are marked with his full name, and should not be confused with Barclay, another maker of very fine costume pieces from the era.

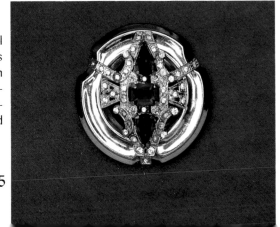

Three McClelland Barclay brooches. The center brooch is a 3" dual layered leaf with separate pave rhinestones regally overlapping its gold counterpart, $225-275. The rectangular silvery blue brooch at the top has a classic Barclay look with its elegant faux sapphires surrounded by pave stones and heavy deco-style base, $300-375. At the bottom is an oval version of the same design in gold with ruby red stones, $300-375.

Eugene

Eugene was originally a designer for Miriam Haskell and later produced his own jewelry under the Eugene name. Of the same genre of design as Haskell, De Mario, and Robert Levy, Eugene pieces are rarely seen today, most probably because many of them are still treasured by their original owners. Additionally, it appears that these designs were available for only a short period of time, with production stopping sometime during the 1960s.

An innovation of design, this Eugene bracelet has four rows in an unusually striking combination of pale blue and green stones, and an elaborate clasp of matching stones in various cuts and sizes. The clasp snaps open to reveal a filigree slide for easy size adjustment, $275-375.

Three pair of earrings with wired beads and multicolored stones. Earrings, top to bottom, $50-65; $35-45; $40-50. Double strand of faux pearls, culminating in an elaborate center drop of gold flowers, pearls, and rhinestones, $175-225. All marked Eugene.

Sarah Coventry

Conceived in 1949 to be sold exclusively at home parties, Sarah Coventry jewelry enjoyed enormous success during the 1950s and 1960s with this superbly timed marketing idea that was uncannily in sync with the atmosphere of postwar America. The boom in housing tracts and an exodus to suburban living created a perfect atmosphere for the home party to flourish.

Although this concept was discontinued in 1984, rights to the Coventry name were later acquired by a Canadian company.

It's worth noting that many Coventry pieces from the 50s-60s era are beautifully executed in bold designs. Unfortunately, however, the name has been too quickly - and unfairly - dismissed

4" floral brooch and earrings have detailed filigree work and accents of fuschia aurora borealis stones, $85-110. Bottom brooch has flowing leaves curling around double rhinestone flower, $50-65. All marked Sarah Coventry, circa 1950-1960s.

The lasting beauty of Sarah Coventry. Left to right: 5" floral brooch with faux topaz center is a symphony of graceful curves, $65-85; pendant is ablaze with brilliant amber and citrine-colored crystals, $60-75; the 3½" bar brooch has the same appeal today as it did decades ago, $50-65.

Fine example of an antique Whiting and Davis delicate mesh purse in original box, marked Patented February 1921, and underneath October 3, 1920, $800+. The cuff bracelet, with huge faux topaz stone, is also by Whiting and Davis, $135-160.

because of this association with the home party venue. As those who attended parties will recall, Coventry jewelry was not considered inexpensive for the average buyer back then and was quite appealing. Consequently, dealers, collectors, and individuals searching for jewelry for their own personal use, would be well advised to take another look. Generally available at modest prices, they can become an inexpensive, eye-catching addition to a showcase-or one's own jewelry box.

Top: Slide bracelet of gold mesh has beautifully engraved center section, $200-275. Center: With its tiny wrist strap, this gold mesh purse is of older vintage, $65-85; gold ring has large luminescent pink stone, $30-50; silver mesh bag has chain handle and rhinestone closure, $50-65. Bottom: delicate cameo rests in center of this gold mesh choker, $65-85. All marked Whiting and Davis.

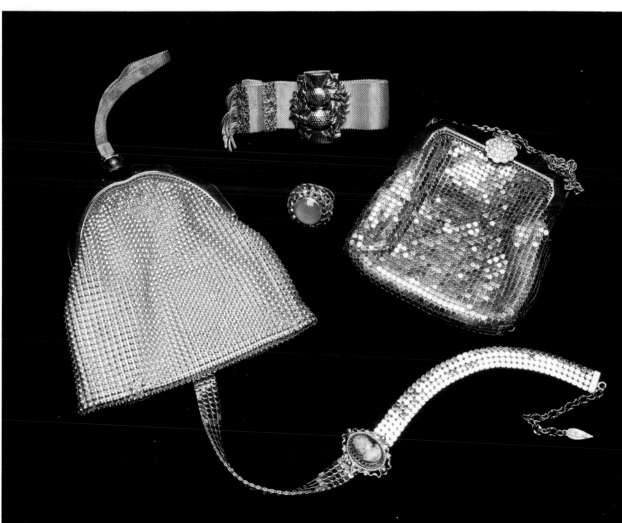

Whiting and Davis

Started in 1876 in Massachusetts, and later doing business at their Attleboro, Massachusetts facilities, Whiting and Davis established their reputation with the design and production of beautiful, finely-woven gold and silver mesh evening bags. Although the styles, understandably, changed over the years, they maintained an almost exclusive position among American purveyors of similar items. Infused with a special aura, these delicate mesh pieces continue to bring pleasure to contemporary women who search for and appreciate the beauty of bygone days.

As an adjunct to this ever-popular business, Whiting and Davis also manufactured distinctive jewelry, which ranged from dainty mesh chokers that transported the wearer to Victorian times to dynamic and showy bracelets, more in keeping with the bold look so popular during the later decades of the 20th century.

Pewter-look bracelet, $250-300, with exquisite detail and giant red center stone rests on silver mesh handbag, $75-100. A polished silver snake cuff completes this trio, $100-125, all by Whiting and Davis.

159

This necklace of gold-plated metal slab links was featured in a 1979 Les Bernard advertisement.

Les Bernard

The company bearing the name Les Bernard, Inc., had as its founder the son of another well-known pioneer of jewelry's golden age. Harold Shapiro was a partner in the Vogue Jewelry operation, and his son, Bernard, following in his illustrious father's footsteps, incorporated Les Bernard in 1963.

The 26-year history of Les Bernard is again a tribute to one father's very positive influence on his son, for Bernard Shapiro has built his own reputation in the complex world of fashion jewelry. In fact, the pinnacle achievement of their twenty-fifth anniversary year was being named the recipient of the coveted 1988 Dallas Fashion Award, just one indication of the respect the Les Bernard organization has achieved in the industry and with their legion of admirers and loyal customers.

Innovation is the watchword of any forward-thinking organization, and Les Bernard has adhered to this rule. As an example, in the late 1960s they added a new dimension to the always popular flower and bird motifs. These brooches had whimsical moveable parts, and costume jewelry buyers, always eager for the new and different, were enchanted.

This "flounder" has been "beached!" Gradations of blue enameling and gold comprise the body, while a pearl eye, pearl and rhinestone accents, and a gold tail complete the seafaring picture. $175-225. On right is a cuff bracelet of pale pink enamel with rhinestone insets, $125-150. Both are marked Les Bernard.

During this same period the Les Bernard line offered a reintroduction of the marcasite jewelry so popular decades before. This time, however, they interspersed sparkling colored stones with the delicate marcasites, creating an effect that was both dazzling and intriguing. The 1960s also brought renewed interest in the popularity of gold-plated sterling, in no small measure the result of new designs in this medium that were offered by Les Bernard. It was a glorious decade for costume jewelry, establishing the company as an innovative force in the industry - a title they wouldn't relinquish in the ensuing years.

This became apparent during the craze for 14-carat gold chains in the 1970s that caused such an upheaval in the fashion jewelry industry in general, but was met head-on by Bernard Shapiro. The company decided to "fight fire with fire" by introducing the "baby chain" look. This not only catered to the desires of customers who refused to pay 14-carat prices, but it also elaborated quite nicely on the "single chain" look - with which, for economic reasons, most women had to be content.

These "nothing chains" of Les Bernard could be worn in groupings of graduated sizes, without "real gold" prices, thereby serving a dual purpose - they conveyed a stronger fashion message than a single chain in 14-carat gold, were unquestionably less expensive, and who but the wearer would know the difference! The fire ignited by this "costume jewelry response" to a "fine jewelry fad" burned brightly, and "baby chains" were another instant success.

Biwi pearls were also a sought-after item during this period, and Les Bernard added many beautiful faux biwi designs to the 1970s lines. Semiprecious materials were also incorporated in pieces featuring tiger's eye, amber, coral, and ivory, helping them to maintain their leadership position in the industry for some eight years.

During the late 1970s and early 1980s, Les Bernard designed and produced jewelry for two renowned couturiers - Mary McFadden and James Galanos - as well as introducing the highly successful Dynasty Collection, an offshoot of the popular TV program. Les Bernard was among the forerunners in the designer licensing concept for fashion jewelry. Later, they added Italian designer Ugo Correani in - as Bernard Shapiro succinctly stated - "a never-ending quest to keep the juices flowing." [9]

The national ad tag line for Les Bernard Jewelry reads, "We select what we offer as carefully as you select what you buy." Jewelry produced by Bernard Shapiro, both past and present, is proof that this credo lives up to its promise - and then some!

[9] From telephone interview with Bernard Shapiro.

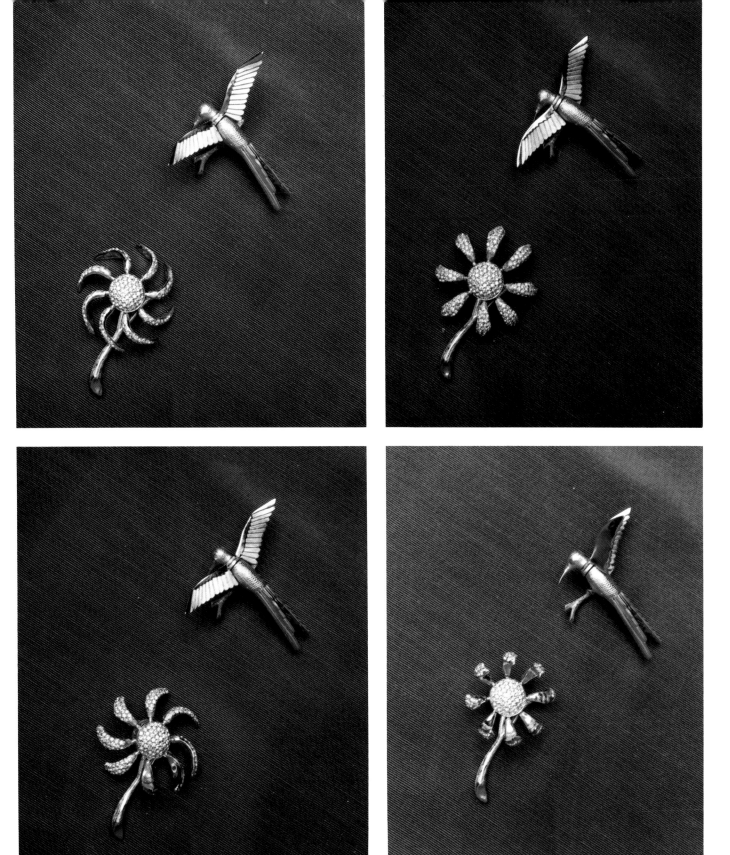

These moveable pieces, courtesy of the Bernard Shapiro family, are indicative of the innovation Les Bernard jewelry brought to the industry when the company was founded in 1962. The bird's wings open and close, $250-325, and the flower's petals adjust at the whim of the wearer, $200-250.

Earrings and a ring, all marked Vogue. Cluster earrings of deep red crystals, $85-100; high-domed ring has blue accents, $40-60; large floral earrings of brilliant green and clear crystals, $95-125; filigreed, double balls rotate on these earrings with delicate enameling and multicolored accents, $110-135.

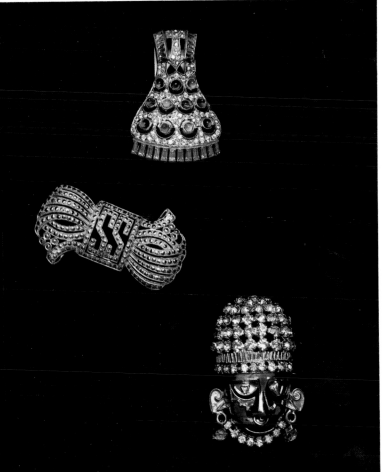

These early Vogue pieces are from the Bernard Shapiro (Les Bernard) family collection, and are representative of the beauty and innovation common to Vogue jewelry. The clip at top, studded with colorful stones, is unusually appealing in both shape and design, $250-300; the initialed center brooch is stunningly Deco in execution, $200-250; the bottom figure has an intriguing combination of Egyptian and blackamoor influences, $300-375.

Vogue

The Vogue Jewelry Novelty Company, as it was originally known, was founded in the 1930s by George Grand. Assisting Grand in marketing, sales, and manufacturing capacities were Jack Gilbert and Harold Shapiro (father of Bernard Shapiro, who would found Les Bernard, Inc., a generation later.)

Even though fashion jewelry sections didn't exist in the department store venue during Vogue's earlier years, these three gentlemen wisely sensed a trend to accessorizing with costume jewelry. Initially catering to the millinery and couturier trade, they supplied costume ornaments to adorn the hats of renowned milliners like Mr. John and Lily Daché, and jewelry pieces for the garments of couturiers like Hattie Carnegie and Nettie Rosenstein.

However, it was a piece of fashion jewelry for a Mr. John hat that launched Vogue's venture into costume jewelry for *everyone*. It all began during World War II when Mr. John attached Vogue's American flag pins to some of his creations. They made such an exciting statement that I. Magnin foresaw a fashion *coup* if the pins could be marketed separately. In an understandable furor of patriotism, the public embraced the idea, and the flag pins became an enormous success. The gentlemen at Vogue wisely concluded that if a hat adornment could be snowballed into a craze for patriotic jewelry, it'd be worthwhile to gamble on the possibility that other designs would tempt the public, as well. How right they were!

In August of 1947, George Grand signed a partnership agreement with Shapiro and Gilbert. Although Grand died the following year, his legacy remained, with Shapiro and Gilbert at the helm. Vogue continued to flourish, meeting customer demands for new and exciting baubles with a spate of innovative ideas. Among these was one of the hottest jewelry items of the 1950s, which Vogue introduced to the American market early in the decade. It was the tin-cut Austrian crystals and beaded ropes, which garnered them the well-deserved title "king of the beaded ropes."

The Shapiros left the Vogue operation in 1962, but the Vogue name continued to dazzle on a smaller scale until the company disbanded in the mid-1970s. Thanks to the design and marketing skills of George Grand, Harold Shapiro, and Jack Gilbert, the Vogue name will always be well worth the search when serious collectors go on their next treasure hunt!

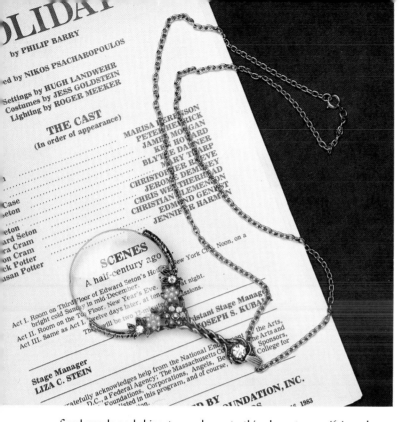

Seed pearls and rhinestones decorate this elegant magnifying glass. Accessocraft was responsible for perfecting the techniques necessary to insert magnifying lenses into intricate jewelry designs, $125-175.

Accessocraft's 4" lapel brooch has the charm of an old-fashioned watch fob, featuring faux lapis stones, the bottom one nestled in a golden "basket," $150-200.

Take your pick! This unique Accessocraft piece can be either a dramatic necklace or stunning belt. Links of "tortoise" and ivory composition are joined by decorative gold pieces. A gold tassel completes the picture, $150-225.

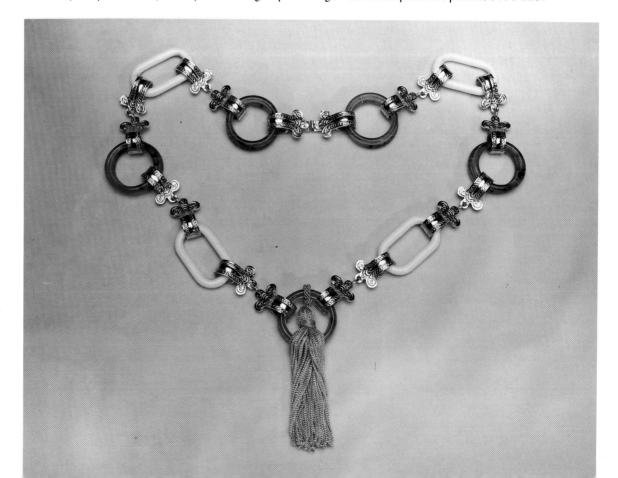

Accessocraft

Accessocraft was founded in the 1930s by Edgar Rodelheimer and Theodore Steinman, who had earlier been a salesman for Monocraft - later Monet.

With the advent of World War II and shortly after their independent entry into the jewelry industry, Accessocraft was responsible for the production of tens of thousands of war relief pins, including the famous British design, with monies raised in this endeavor contributed to charity. However, the team of Steinman and Rodelheimer retained the

This hefty Accessocraft pendant has a heraldic theme and is attached to four strands of heavy gold chain. $135-175

tools and dies for these masterpieces, and they remained a part of the Accessocraft firm until its dissolution, as did original French parts for jewelry items of the Victorian and antique-look genre.

Accessocraft established an enviable reputation for unusual jewelry design and skill of execution, including the introduction of elaborate magnifying glass necklaces and opera glasses, all crafted with optical glass and many featuring Art Nouveau designs and dazzling rhinestone ropes. They were the originators of cobra belts, and in the late 1970s their business evolved into producing ornaments for decorative handbags and shoe buckles. Accessocraft was also the top manufacturer of Chanel-type chain belts and overbelts with buckles.

During its long history, the company was associated with the Pauline Trigere jewelry line and in original belt and jewelry designs for Anne Klein who, before her death, worked closely with them in supervising the production of these pieces. In order to maintain the quality and integrity of the finished product, Accessocraft insisted on direct input from those with whom they collaborated, and their relationship with the late Anne Klein was a most productive one.

Paul Steinman, Theodore's son, was associated with the Accessocraft firm for over 30 years, serving as president for twenty. The Accessocraft operation came to an end in 1996 when they could no longer occupy the site of their long-standing suburban New York factory.

Pennino

Although an outstanding "golden age" contributor, background information on Pennino is, unfortunately, vague. We do know that the talented Benedetto Panetta was a designer and model maker for early Pennino, following a stint with the Trifari operation. By the most rigid of standards, Pennino ranks among the "best of the best" in costume jewelry from the past.

Top: Sterling silver Pennino brooch has lacy design, studded with blue stones and pave rhinestones. Matching earrings duplicate this delicate pattern, $175-250 (set). At bottom is a Pennino brooch in heavy goldplating, with clear blue crystals forming the leaves of this magnificent jeweled tree, $200-275.

Pennino at its finest in this exquisite rhinestone necklace, with rigid overlapping center section, $800+.

Castlecliff

Founded in the 1940s by Clifford Furst, with William Markle as its chief designer, Castlecliff left an indelible mark on the costume jewelry industry. The beauty of each piece made these treasures just as prized by women then as by those lucky enough to discover the Castlecliff logo on a piece of vintage jewelry today.

Sold in only the finest stores, the Castlecliff line featured bold and stylized designs, many of which reflected Markle's architectural background. Although production of Castlecliff ended in the 1960s, today we can admire not only their jewelry from this golden age, but the nostalgic print ads that appeared in major fashion magazines of the time.

Four fine examples of jewelry marked Castlecliff. Mythological horse holds reins in his teeth to form clasp of this unusual bracelet, $145-175; enameled bird perches on spray of red rhinestone flowers, $85-125, while striated angel trumpets a yuletide message, $50-65. At bottom is sterling silver heart with arrow piercing its brilliant red center, $85-125.

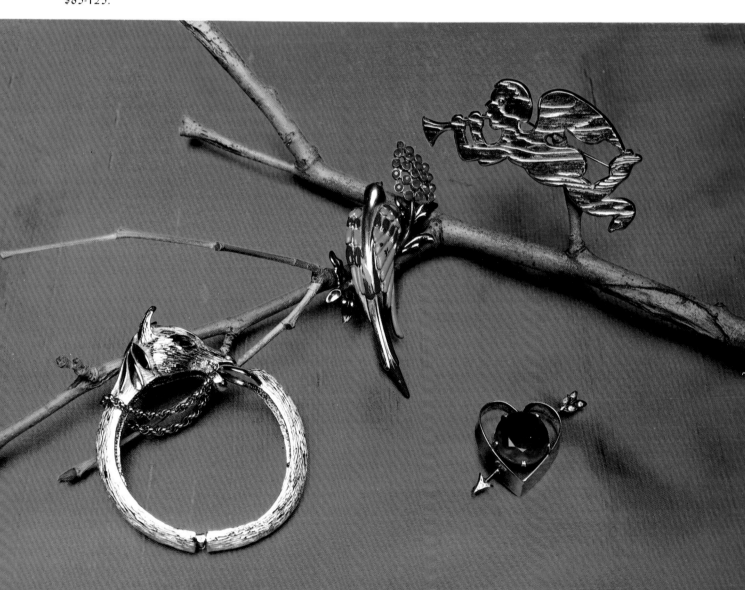

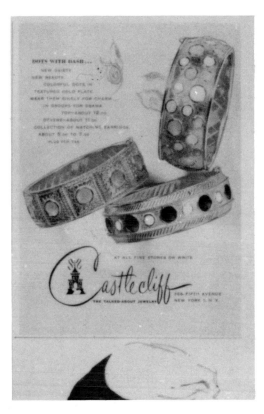

This Castlecliff ad is from the March 1954 issue of *Harper's Bazaar*.

A graceful Castlecliff design of tremendous beauty. Golden tendrils curl around the pave rhinestone center. A real "show stopper," $125-175.

A Castlecliff masterpiece. Burnished tendrils studded with brilliant rhinestones encapsulate a giant faux topaz in this 3" brooch that rises to a depth of 1", $350-550.

Krementz

Founded in 1884, the Krementz jewelry business remains in operation today in Newark, New Jersey. Best known for its dainty designs, many featuring tiny raised flowers and utilizing a decades-old special rolled-gold process, these pieces are very distinctive in appearance and easily recognizable. Although totally removed from the "glitz and glitter" for which this era was most remembered, this unique jewelry has enormous appeal, and it's understandable why there are so many devoted Krementz collectors.

With their delicate look and layered flowers, these pieces are examples of the special techniques and fine workmanship for which Krementz is famous. Top to bottom: Circle brooch in pink and regular gold finish, $40-60. Middle: Matching bracelet, $50-75, and earrings, $20-30. Bottom: brooch of larger flowers, $40-60.

Courtesy of Monet archives, New York.

Monet jewelry from the 1940s. Courtesy of Monet archives, New York.

Monet

Founded by brothers Jay and Michael Chernow in 1937, Monet jewelry was the outgrowth of a business called Monocraft that initially supplied monograms for handbags. Since this involved an in-depth knowledge of design and metalwork not unlike that necessary for jewelry production, it was a natural transition for these brothers to turn their business and artistic acumen to the jeweler's trade. Undoubtedly the ensuing 60-plus years have far surpassed the Chernow's greatest expectations, for the business was launched at a most auspicious time. The world was on the brink of changes of unexpected magnitude, and those changes would be reflected in every aspect of daily life, including fashion and accessorizing.

Since 1937, this ever-changing face of fashion required shifting priorities and constant innovation. Monet's imaginative designers have continually met that challenge with jewelry that excites and revitalizes. They recognized the swiftly changing economic and social scene and created jewelry to reflect it - and American women have been enthusiastic about the results. For instance, in the 1940s many designs were influenced by the military aura of World War II, while at the same time others reflected the romantic escapism of Hollywood films. Fashions swung from wide-shouldered suits and straight skirts in the wartime years to the revolution created by Dior's "New Look" later in the decade.

It was during this dichotomous period, when the fashion world was undergoing a revolution of sorts, that Monet emerged as a costume jewelry leader in the United States. Many of those first designs were in the form of ensembles, some utilizing sterling silver and brilliantly faceted stones. Even the equestrian theme, still popular today, was an important selling feature.

In the 1950s Monet concentrated on uncluttered pieces like graceful sterling bow pins. Nevertheless, the youthful audience had their own special needs, and Monet's designers reacted with poodle pins, charm bracelets, and other whimsical pieces to appeal to the younger set.

Monet jewelry became bolder in the 1960s, reflecting more daring fashions and an upsurge in pop-art creativity. Colors were bolder and skirts were shorter, and Monet's designers responded with hoop earrings, big pendants, and bangles.

With this 60-year history of successfully adapting to constantly changing images, it's not surprising that Monet remains a "giant," in both quality and quantity, of the very volatile and competitive costume jewelry industry.

The sterling bows are dynamic in this 1950s photo. Courtesy of Monet archives, New York.

Top to bottom: Gold cuff has giant pearl center with rhinestone accents, $60-75; whimsical cat with emerald green eyes, $40-65; spider brooch has Art Moderne influence, $30-40; bracelet of dual burnished links, $35-45. All marked Monet.

1960's Monet jewelry. Courtesy of Monet archives, New York.

Jewelry by Monet from the 1970s. Courtesy of Monet archives, New York.

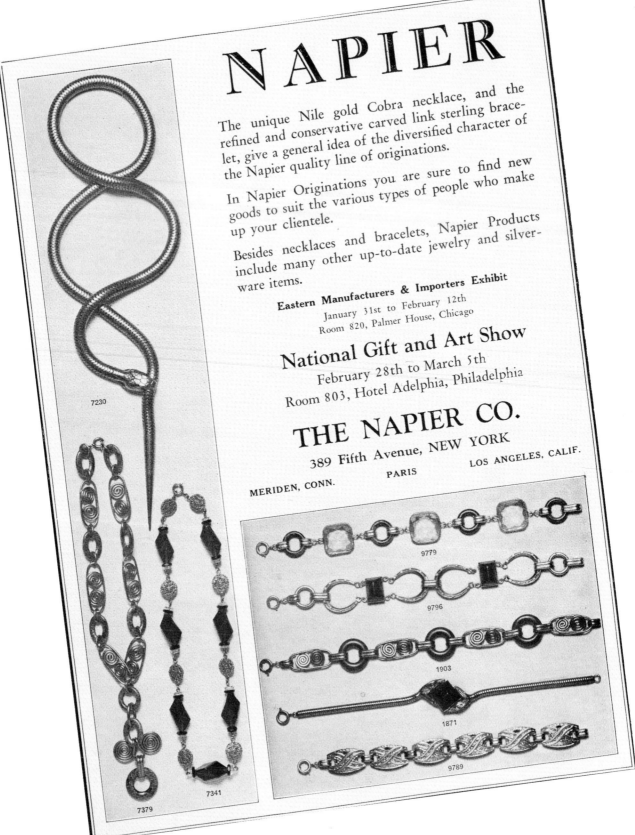

NAPIER

The unique Nile gold Cobra necklace, and the refined and conservative carved link sterling bracelet, give a general idea of the diversified character of the Napier quality line of originations.

In Napier Originations you are sure to find new goods to suit the various types of people who make up your clientele.

Besides necklaces and bracelets, Napier Products include many other up-to-date jewelry and silverware items.

Eastern Manufacturers & Importers Exhibit
January 31st to February 12th
Room 820, Palmer House, Chicago

National Gift and Art Show
February 28th to March 5th
Room 803, Hotel Adelphia, Philadelphia

THE NAPIER CO.
389 Fifth Avenue, NEW YORK

MERIDEN, CONN.   PARIS   LOS ANGELES, CALIF.

Advertisement from *The Gift and Art Shop* magazine for February, 1927. Courtesy of The Napier Company.

176

Napier

The Napier Company began as Whitney and Rice in North Attleboro, Massachusetts in 1875, later changed its name to Carpenter and Bliss, then the Bliss Company, and finally became Napier in 1922. Until it was, unfortunately, forced to close the doors of its Meriden, Connecticut operation in October of 1999, their lengthy history made Napier the oldest fashion jewelry house in the United States. And an illustrious history it was!

When the company moved to Meriden in 1890, they were responsible for producing the first ornamental glass in America, an interesting addition to their basic jewelry line. Not content with one "first," Napier's subsidiary, the Meriden Sterling Company, accomplished another by pioneering the manufacture of sterling silver merchandise in what soon became known as The Silver City.

In 1914 James Napier began his association with the Bliss Company and served as general manager during a time when production facilities were converted to aid the war effort. Mr. Napier headed the company for 45 years, until his sudden death in 1960. He was a guiding force in its phenomenal growth, which was interrupted only once following World War I, this time by World War II, when war materials were again manufactured at the plant instead of fashion jewelry.

Although the Napier Company had been a mainstay of Meriden for over one hundred years, their longevity is startlingly clarified when one discoveres that they had maintained showrooms in various locations on New York's Fifth Avenue for nearly as long.

During their beginnings in North Attleboro, Napier produced jewelry items of the day, like watch chains and chatelaines. In the ensuing century, those watch chains and chatelaines progressed to cobra necklaces and Egyptian pieces in the 1920s and 1930s, and fan jewelry in the 1950s - with a percentage of the profits from the latter contributed to the Children's Memorial Cancer Fund. Enormous cuff bracelets, smashing bibs and "over the ear" clips were just some of the items that rounded out the "golden age."

Napier enthusiasts, like costume jewelry lovers everywhere, encompass a broad spectrum of the American scene. In the 1950s, Napier presented First Lady Mamie Eisenhower with a specially designed elephant bracelet, a favorite piece that she wore almost daily. Turning their attention to another generation, the 1955 Miss America Pageant program reveals that *all* the contestants (including Miss America herself), the semifinalists, and those otherwise honored received fashion jewelry by The Napier Company.

Just as Mamie Eisenhower and the young ladies in Atlantic City treasured their Napier creations, so, too, have millions of other women, past and present. Although we can no longer look forward to Napier's Meriden, Connecticut creations, their jewelry from years past will always be an important part of every jewelry enthusiast's collection. Napier leaves behind a proud tradition of nearly 125 years. They will be sorely missed!

Delicately-sculptured golden leaves have been artfully gathered into an adjustable necklace, cuff bracelet, and matching earclips by Napier. Courtesy The Napier Company.

Pear-shaped iridescent crystal enhances delicate golden strands, forming this necklace and earclips by Napier. Courtesy The Napier Company.

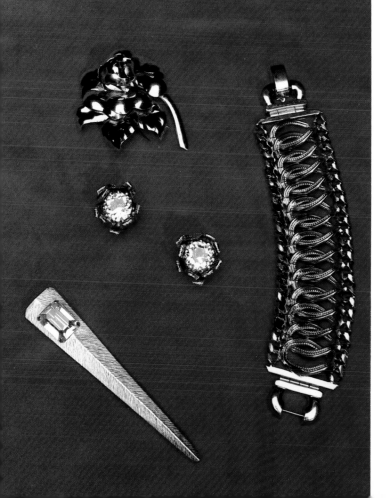

Napier vermeil fur clip has raised floral center, circa 1930s or early 1940s, $125-155; high petals reveal brilliant blue centers on these Napier earrings, $35-50; tailored Di Nicola brooch with faux citrine center stone, $50-65; Bergere bracelet of heavy, woven links, $50-75.

178

Bergere

Founded in the late 1940s as Herbert and Pohs, and now seen infrequently, Bergere pieces were always interesting and well-constructed. This popular line of upscale jewelry continued to be produced into the 1960s.

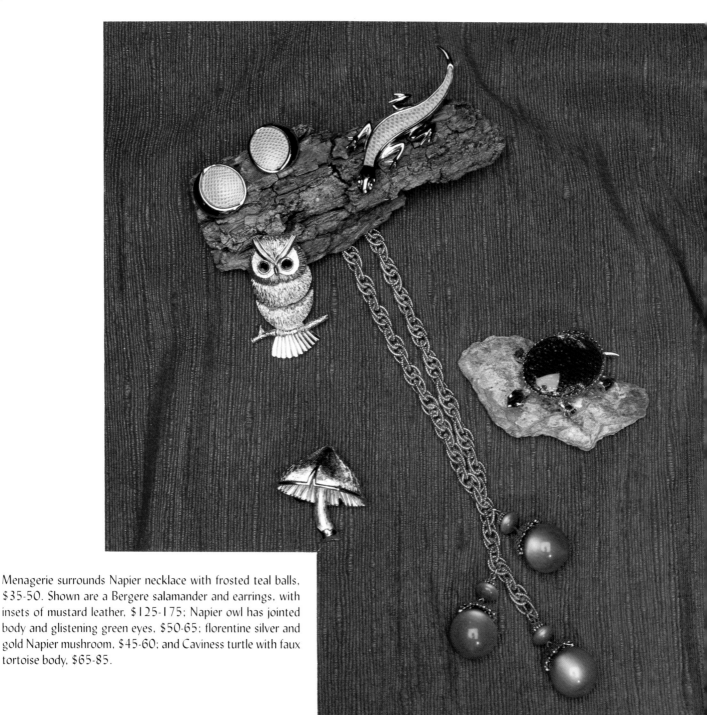

Menagerie surrounds Napier necklace with frosted teal balls, $35-50. Shown are a Bergere salamander and earrings, with insets of mustard leather, $125-175; Napier owl has jointed body and glistening green eyes, $50-65; florentine silver and gold Napier mushroom, $45-60; and Caviness turtle with faux tortoise body, $65-85.

Sandor

Founded in the late 1930s or early 1940s by Sandor Goldberger, Sandor was considered a prime innovator during this era and is credited with being one of the first to offer enameling in costume designs. These pieces, some marked Sandor Goldberger and other simply Sandor, were of very high quality and are found only infrequently, making them very desirable amid today's ever dwindling inventory of prime vintage jewelry. The Sandor operation closed its doors in the mid-1970s.

Top to bottom: enameled flower with single red stone nestled in center, $65-85; floral domed earrings of pale blue enamel interspersed with tiny rhinestones, $40-55; sterling silver bow has center flower and raised leaves with red "berries," $275-375; burnished gold brooch features large brown center stone in unusual design, $45-65. All marked Sandor.

This massive necklace with its garland of enameled flowers carries the jewelers art to new heights. Its design and execution are a testimonial to Sandor's status as one of the "greats" in vintage costume jewelery. $400-600

Di Nicola

Another fine quality line of the era, Di Nicola was founded by Jerry Di Nicola in the late 1950s or early 1960s and became part of the Capri jewelry company during the last five years of its existence. Pieces bearing the Di Nicola name have not been made since the early 1970s, and remain scarce for collectors.

Mosell

Founded in 1940 as Frederick Mosell Jewelry, Mosell is another name at the forefront of design excellence and quality that is, unfortunately, also rarely seen today.

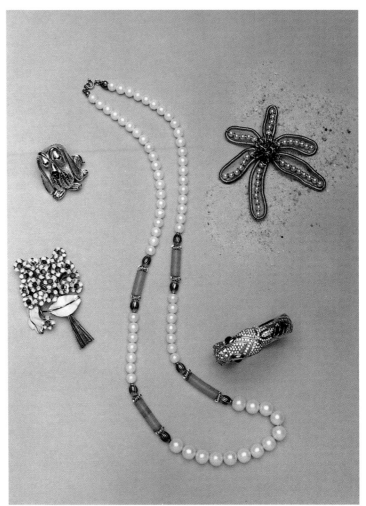

Soulful dog marked Panetta, $55-75. Sterling flower by Sandor, $175-250. Necklace of faux pearls with layers of frosted tan discs and gold rondels, marked Di Nicola, $65-85. Napier starfish is of flexible mesh with pearl inserts and sparkling blue center, $50-75. Snake cuff marked Di Nicola has green cabochon eyes and is studded with pave rhinestones, $135-175.

Two fine designers are represented in this grouping. Brushed gold bow marked Panetta is edged in pave rhinestones, $125-150; in forefront is elegant Mosell brooch of faux pearls and center green cabochon, with matching earrings, $275-350.

Is it or isn't it? The design and stately elegance of this magnificent necklace would make any wearer proud, and any bystander envious, $300-500. Courtesy of Panetta Jewelry.

This parure of large faux amethysts with links of glittering diamond-like stones is a stunning example of the flawless beauty for which Panetta is justifiably renowned, $600+. Courtesy of Panetta Jewelry.

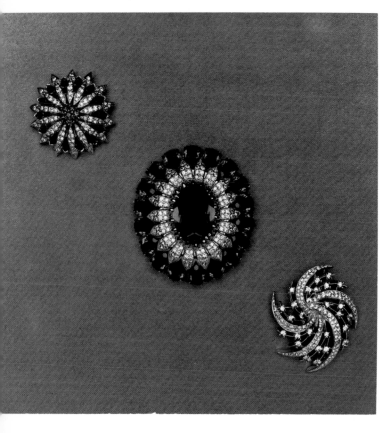

The "authentic look" is supremely evident in these three Panetta brooches, glimmering with faux sapphires, $145-185, faux amethysts, $175-250, and rhinestones, $175-225. Courtesy of Panetta Jewelry.

182

Panetta

A tradition of quality and the *real look* in fine costume jewelry...that has been the hallmark of Panetta jewelry since it was established in New York City in 1945. The Panetta magic started many years before, however, when Benedetto Panetta began his career as a jeweler and designer, specializing in hand-crafted platinum jewelry at his shop in Naples, Italy.

Financial reverses and family illness played a major role in Panetta's emigration to the United States in 1909. His expertise was immediately recognized, and for many years he worked exclusively as a platinum jeweler. The Great Depression, with its devastating effects on the economy, caused Panetta to expand his skills into the utilization of white metals. It was a decision he never regretted since, because of his experience in working with platinum, he was able to bring a look of brilliant authenticity to costume pieces. In an industry that was rapidly expanding, his skills became a precious commodity, with many costume jewelry manufacturers vying for his talents. Trifari emerged the victor, and Benedetto Panetta became one of their chief modelmakers, contributing to the early, highly stylized and beautiful Trifari designs eagerly searched for today.

When Trifari moved their facilities from New York to Providence, Rhode Island, in the 1930s, Panetta chose not to uproot his family, opting instead to continue his modelmaking and designing skills with another highly regarded jewelry maker, Pennino Brothers. Trifari, Pennino, and later his own company, Panetta Jewelry - Benedetto Panetta's skillful hands and creative mind contributed to the exquisite costume jewelry produced by all three of these *golden age* giants. Few have equaled this enviable achievement, either before or since!

It was during the grim depression period that Panetta's sons, Armand and Amadeo, were serving an apprenticeship under Benedetto Panetta's patient tutelage, spending countless weekends and long hours after their regular high school academics laboriously mastering their father's trade. A more dedicated or demanding teacher could not have been found - nor two pupils more eager to learn! Amadeo Panetta recalls that those times of careful preparation were guided by his father's explicit credo: *quality and beauty.*

When Amadeo and Armand Panetta began their independent careers, Armand worked as a diamond setter while Amadeo's major skill was in modelmaking. Both, however, had received a thorough apprenticeship in every aspect of jewelry making, from design to modelmaking to stonesetting.

Delayed by the intrusion of World War II and the time both sons spent in service to their country, the credo of quality and beauty eventually became the cornerstone of a fledging company, aptly named Panetta Jewelry, when the father and his two sons became equal partners in a venture of their own at war's end. Well rounded in all aspects of the business, Armand specifically converted his abilities as a diamond setter to the *real look* in costume pieces. Amadeo continued his expertise in modelmaking, and Benedetto Panetta contributed his lifetime of experience! Thus, the company became a natural outgrowth of the combined talents of all three. The dazzling results of this rigorous background of perfection in the jeweler's art, which had been passed on from father to sons, were immediately recognized by peers and public alike.

Starting with very little capital, the Panetta family chose to maintain a small, exclusive image featuring original designs hand-set in sterling silver. Later they also worked in white metal, creating a finished product that was no less inspired, with the modulation and interpretation of design only growing in distinction.

Every operation was completed on-premise by master craftsmen, and only authentic-looking designs were considered worthy of the Panetta logo. Their exclusive plating process has been aptly named *two toning* and involves the incorporation of both gold and rhodium. For over half a century, Panetta jewelry equaled and frequently exceeded the look of their platinum and gold counterparts, and it is not surprising that many affluent clients have chosen to wear Panetta designs instead of precious jewelry.

Although Benedetto Panetta died in the 1960s, Amadeo and Armand continued the tradition this talented trio established in 1945. They are justifiably proud that Panetta employees learned or expertly honed their skills through their association with the company, in much the same way that Benedetto Panetta taught his sons. Each recognized that to compromise these standard would lead to the dissolution of what is already in danger of becoming legend rather than ongoing reality. The loss of dedicated craftsmen and those, like the Panettas, who willingly shared their knowledge, would deal a severe blow to an industry that has brought great pleasure to many- and established itself in the annals of design and workmanship, regardless of the medium. To have these skills become a "lost art" in the future is an unthinkable possibility to those who labored so diligently on its behalf.

During the height of the depression, Benedetto Panetta's succinct advice to his sons was "You have to learn a trade. If you learn a trade you'll never starve." By his actions he added another unspoken credo. Simply stated, it is *When a trade is learned, and learned well and without compromise, you will have pride that lasts a lifetime - and its results will bear fruit long beyond.*

Learn a trade. Never compromise on quality or beauty. Share your knowledge. Those fortunate enough to have heeded these examples by thought and deed will, in turn, have gained a measure of immortality. Benedetto Panetta was indeed a very wise man!

A gigantic brooch of faux emeralds and topaz, $275-375, is surrounded by elegant drop earrings with a delicate Victorian ambiance, top: $150-175; bottom: $175-225. Courtesy of Panetta Jewelry.

Whimsy and beauty combine in a sultry peacock and undulating salamander, $350-500 ea. The triple-tiered gold brooch is topped with a giant faux onyx stone, $200-275. Courtesy of Panetta Jewelry.

Opposite:
These sensational bracelets could fool any eye, from the Deco beauty of geometric "diamonds", $250-350, to a single strand of glittering precious and semiprecious "look-alikes", $225-300. Courtesy of Panetta Jewelry.

These pieces show the wide range of designs produced under the Florenza name. Left: Large starfish brooch, $95-135, and another floral filigree brooch, $45-65. Center: massive necklace with mythological motif, $200-250. Right: enamel and gold frog is a deceiving creature, for he's actually a tape measure, $50-65.

These Florenza pieces are fine examples of their antique "Victorian" look. The brooch has delicate filigree work, with faux garnets and turquoise, and an old-fashioned center cameo, $75-110; although large, the bracelet exhibits the same qualities, with intaglio cameo insets, $150-200.

Two jewel boxes, one with brilliantly encrusted top, $95-145, the other of white enamel with large blue center stone, $65-85; a large fleur de lis brooch, $95-135, presents a striking contrast to the delicate Victorian-look bar pin, $65-85 ea. All marked Florenza.

Florenza

Florenza is a jewel in the crown of costume jewelry masterpieces. Sold only to wholesalers worldwide, the company was started in the mid-1940s by Daniel Kasoff as Dan Kasoff, Inc., the company responsible for the design copyright of Florenza. Located for a short time on 28th Street in New York, the operation was relocated to 31st Street in 1945, where it remained for nearly 40 years, expanding as its business increased.

Involved in the jewelry industry since childhood, Dan's son Lawrence joined Dan Kasoff, Inc. on a full-time basis in 1956. Larry Kasoff continued there until the factory was forced to close in 1981 as the result of injuries he suffered in an automobile accident, and his father's inability to continue to manage the business he had started so many years before.

Florenza pieces, which include not only jewelry but dainty boutique items like enameled and jewel-encrusted boxes, are very distinctive. Many have the look of turn-of-the-century Victorian designs, with antique settings and finishes replete with stones that mimic the "real" thing. It's interesting to look at these renditions now and realize that they were not only popular when produced, but captured an even later trend -- the resurgence of interest in the Victorian "look" during the closing decades of the 20th century. Florenza was also responsible for perfecting three original finishes - French gold, French rose, and Wedgewood - each of which added yet another facet to the appealing ambiance of this very distinctive jewelry.

This exquisite Florenza parure, with its intricate layered design, is a delightful contrast of colors and applications. The cream-colored enamel base enhances the unusual array of pastel stones and delicate accents, $175-225.

Top to bottom: Florenza frame of faux peridots and amethysts, $125-175; lavender and green brooch and earrings have delicate stones and enameling, $85-115; shades of lavender and periwinkle abound on this large Florenza brooch that also can be worn as a pendant, $175-225; frosted and aurora stones in an unusual combination of colors create a very Victorian look on another Florenza piece, $75-115.

Cadoro

Cadora was established by Steve Brody, a former actor, and Dan Steneskieu, a direct descendant of Rumanian royalty who escaped from his native country during World War II. Jet-setters and bon vivants, Brody and Steneskieu imparted a special ambiance to the jewelry business with their distinctive personalities.

Their travels enabled Brody and Steneskieu to personally obtain the finest materials from European suppliers, as well as many of their core designs, which were then adapted to the tastes of the American market. Their insistence on offering only the finest costume jewelry to American women is evident when one discovers a piece of Cadoro today.

When Steneskieu died tragically in the mid-1970s, Brody acquired another partner, but unfortunately the business continued for only a few more years and ceased operations in the early 1980s.

The Cadoro name continues to be held in high esteem, not only by collectors, but also those in the jewelry industry who still remember these gentlemen with fondness and respect.

Simple yet dramatic, this Cadoro pearl necklace has one rhinestone studded gold ball, $150-175; Cadoro cuff bracelet is peppered with faux lapis and turquoise stones, $145-195; triple strand of Deltah pearls has showy center accent of pearls and rhinestones, $125-150.

Hollycraft

The company responsible for Hollycraft jewelry was founded by Joseph Chorbajian in the early 1940s as Hollywood Jewelry. A survivor of the Turkish massacre, Chorbajian emigrated to the United States in 1917, where he remained until his death in 1991 at the age of 91. Joined in the business by Jack Hazard and his cousin Archie, the company was initially located on Broadway in New York City, later moving to 37th Street. After fifty years in the design and production of glorious jewelry, Hollycraft was sold in 1972 and disbanded a few years later.

Avidly sought by collectors, Hollycraft pieces are generally recognizable by their antique finishes and colorful pastel stones of varying sizes and shapes. Although this eye-appealing, pastel melange is most often associated with the Hollycraft name, Chorbajian also created equally magnificent designs incorporating only clear crystals and rhinestones. Along with the Hollycraft logo, most pieces are dated, which is a definite plus for collectors. What a great help to all "golden age" aficionados if other makers from this era had done the same!

These Hollycraft pieces show the variety of colors, shapes, and designs for which Hollycraft is justifiably renowned. The elaborate parure on left is a feast for the eyes, $400-600; opposite is a brooch and earrings set in a subtle combination of mauve and pink with green enameling, $135-185; the wide cuff bracelet is a bolder piece than usually found, $200-300.

Art

The Art jewelry line was founded in the 1940s by Arthur Pepper and only merchandised through wholesalers. Produced in fairly large quantities, with some marked Art and others ModeArt, their offerings ran the gamut - from the look of fine Victorian jewelry to figural and novelty motifs of simpler design. Always interesting and indicative of the era, Art pieces are well worth looking for, with most available at modest cost. The company, like many of its contemporaries, disbanded in the 1970s.

Two very opposite yet equally beautiful pieces by Art: a graceful bird in an interesting combination of antiqued silver and gold, $50-65, and an elegant cluster of faux pearls interspersed with gold, $50-65.

Below: Hollycraft raspberry ring, $50-75. Pastel stones, a Hollycraft trademark, form a delicately lovely bracelet, $145-175; this Hollycraft ring is studded with faux amethysts in a burnished setting, $65-85; a charming "turn of the century" look in this brooch of faux garnets, turquoise and pearls, marked Art, $75-100; an Art figural piece presents a lovely profile, complete with hoop earring, $65-75.

Opposite page, bottom left:
Brooch of amethyst-colored stones of varied sizes and shapes, with matching earrings, marked Beau Jewels, $145-175. In front is a rhinestone brooch with unusual curved design, marked Pell, $95-125.

Pell

Pell was founded in 1941 by four brothers - Bill, Tony, Joe, and Alfred Gaita. World War II forced them to suspend operations very shortly thereafter, resuming production again in the mid-1940s. Earlier jewelry by Pell was primarily of clear rhinestones, many featuring unusual figural subjects in designs that continue to attract attention today.

More recently, the youngest brother, Alfred Gaita, continued producing jewelry under the Pell name in his Brooklyn factory, concentrating mostly on tailored gold pieces and gold with pearls.

Reja

Founded in the 1940s by Sol Finkelstein, Reja designs were of high fashion with an aura of elegance indicative of the most glamorous side of this period, but they are not remembered in much detail by most individuals remaining in the "trade." This is probably because they were produced in smaller quantities than other "giants" of the era and offered primarily in boutique environments.

Reja has not been marketed since the 1960s, and pieces are only sparsely seen today.

Enameled flower with rhinestone accents and blue stamens, $145-185; blue crystal earrings, $50-65, layers of brilliant clear crystals create an outstandingly lovely brooch, $150-200; gold filigree brooch with rhinestone edging in an artfully understated design, $100-135. All marked Reja.

Warner

Founded and operated solely by Joseph Warner, Warner pieces featured brilliant rhinestones, both white and colored, and outstanding floral and insect designs. Since much of their jewelry employed the distinctive "black" backing known as japanning, they are easily recognizable and a unique addition to any collection.

Of the high quality one would generally expect from this period, Warner jewelry has not been marketed for several decades.

Warner and Wiesner pieces create a "rhapsody in blue." Top to bottom: pearls and grey rhinestones stud this compact with matching lipstick holder, $100-125, marked Trickettes by Wiesner, circa 1950s; brilliant blue high-domed brooch with japanned backing marked Warner, $85-100; quality of workmanship is apparent in this heavy Wiesner bracelet and necklace, $145-185; Warner aurora circle earrings, $35-45. At left: brilliant rhinestone circular brooch marked Warner, $65-85; dagger brooch is marked Joseph Wiesner, $135-175.

It's the berries! A Warner raspberry pin, $45-60, and two J.J. strawberries, $30-35 ea., are accompanied by a gigantic, glimmering Warner butterfly, $165-225. All have the charming black finishes that give most Warner pieces a very distinctive and easily recognizable look.

Rader

As the daughter of a jewelry store owner, Pauline Rader's attraction to the medium was an intergral part of her early life. Starting with supplying custom-made pearl designs for another company, Rader was intent on gaining personal and artistic independence by establishing her own business. She did just that in 1962.

Created only for private clients and the boutique venue, Rader's designs most often reflected her fascination with antique pieces she observed in her European travels, and she employed the skills of European craftsmen and New York model makers to bring them to reality. These conceptualized designs ranged from massive animal pendants and elaborate animal brooches to smaller but equally unusual pieces, frequently incorporating enamel with delicate stonework.

Rader was solely responsible for the design of jewelry bearing her logo, placing her apart from many other jewelry operations of the day. Never offered through the general department store trade, pieces bearing her name are particularly noteworthy to those searching for the best and most innovative in vintage costume jewelry.

Caviness

Alice Caviness began her career in the garment industry, but was also encouraged to expand her talents under the guidance of Alfeo Verreccia of Craftsman/Gemcraft. Founded in 1945, and later joined by a partner, Lois Stevens, the Caviness jewelry operation was geared to specialty shop designs. Stevens continued with the business following the death of its founder in 1983.

Triple strands of unusual faux pearls in a flat design, with spacers of grey and aurora borealis crystal stones are featured in this necklace, with dynamic matching cuff bracelet, $250-375. Marked Alice Caviness.

With enameled shell and rhinestone body with gold accents, this charming brooch by Pauline Rader elevates even the lowly snail to the status of a sophisticated figural. $100-150.

Pauline Rader created a bold nautical statement in her own version of "anchors aweigh." The 5" anchor is permanently wrapped with chain and attached to a dangling 2" tassel, causing it to hang slightly askew in a rather intriguing fashion, $145-195.

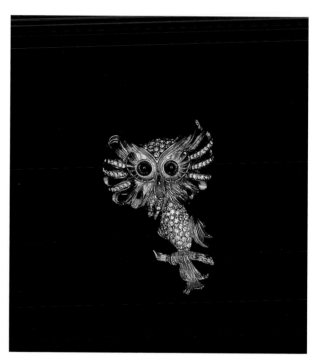

Pauline Rader's owl, with it's startled look, is delightfully amusing and indicative of the range of Rader's design acumen, $150-185.

Muted shades of chartreuse create an unusual rope of sparkling balls and crystal beads, with metallic and filigree accents, $125-175. The brooch and earrings are layered with spinning silver and sequinned crystals on a burnished filigree base, $100-135. Three crystal strands in shades ranging from violet to pale lavender create a striking bib necklace, with matching earrings, $125-150. All marked Alice Caviness.

N. Buckley

Nadja Buckley was a designer of elegant jewelry and accessories during the 1940s. Available in only the finest stores and boutiques, her pieces often featured gold-washed sterling and semi-precious gems in eye-catching settings. Even Buckley's rings were massive - and fabulous. Although opulent and showy, her designs could easily be mistaken for the *real* thing, a rather daring concept in the 1940s! Buckley pieces are rarely seen today - so anyone fortunate enough to own or stumble across one of these "gems" should *hold on for dear life!*

Schreiner

Schreiner jewelry was founded in 1951 by Henry Schreiner, a gentleman who began his career with a company that manufactured shoe buckles during the heyday of the "roaring Twenties." Henry's daughter and son-in-law, Terry and Ambrose Albert, were active in all facets of the operation, with Ambrose Albert responsible for some of Schreiner's most intricate designs. Following Henry Schreiner's death in 1954, the Alberts propelled the fledgling business to even greater heights. Magnificent jeweled belts and buttons were important adjuncts to their business, and Schreiner pieces were included in the jewelry and accessories lines of the couture houses of Norman Norell, Dior, and Adele Simpson.

In 1975, after more than 20 years of offering jewelry items that must be ranked among the finest of the genre, the Schreiner operation was disbanded. Carefully executed and never mass-produced, it's understandable why some individuals focus their entire vintage jewelry collecting only on Schreiner designs.

From the Feb. 1945 issue of *Harper's Bazaar*, this feature page shows that the "finer things" weren't put aside by the tribulations of World War II. Note No. 5, a vermeil Nadja Buckley cigarette box studded with zircons, which Bonwit Teller offered for $900- a hefty sum today, but far dearer in 1945. (Note that No. 6 is by Eisenberg.)

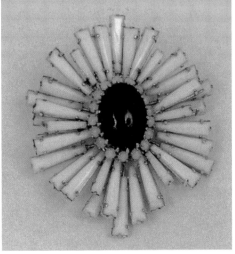

Seen from two vantage points, this brooch is a breathtaking example of the astounding quality of Schreiner designs. Called the "ruffle" brooch, it is 3.5" wide, with a domed black and yellow center sitting atop a double layer of white keystones. An Ambrose Albert design, it was executed on a two-level cast setting. Prohibitive to duplicate today, the model alone would cost an estimated $1,000+, and the keystones, once produced in Germany by Czechoslovakian craftsmen, are no longer available.
From "Materpieces of Costume Jewelry" by Ball and Torem. *Photographs by Dorothy Torem.*

Jeanne

Referred to as "Jeannie" and no longer in production, this jewelry was offered to the public in the boutique venue. Replete with fanciful interpretations of natural subjects, such as fruit, bugs, and butterflies, this is a "fun" line that combines good quality and beauty with designs that often bring a smile to the face - and individuality to any outfit. Logically, Jeanne pieces are not seen with the same regularity as those of many larger producers from this period, making them an even more attractive "find."

Six Jeanne brooches show wide range of unusual designs. Rear: stippled "tomato" with row of jade green "seeds", $65-85; gold bug with marbleized center, $45-65; heavy gold butterfly has pearl and colored stone accents, $125-150. Center: three-dimensional gold angel holding floral bouquet, $65-85. Bottom: lion's head brooch has tangled mane of intricate gold loops, $50-65; rooster departs from usual "barnyard" look in this graceful design, $60-75.

Volupte

Founded in 1926, Volupte is probably best remembered for its elegant compacts. However, their jewelry was of very fine quality and also quite beautiful. It is rarely seen today.

Volupte necklace and earrings feature unusual color combinations, making this an especially attractive set, $350-450. Large faux citrine stones provide sharp contrast to the flat stones that take on deep green, blue, and black tones. In background is Volupte compact, with interesting bar slide for opening and closing, $50-65.

Freirich

Although Freirich was a large operation, especially in the 1960s, their jewelry was later produced on a smaller scale. In addition to supplying modestly-priced jewelry under their own name, Freirich also manufactured high-quality pieces for numerous fashion designers. Starting in 1987, the line carried the name Arthur David.

Two dramatic examples by Reinad are strong evidence of the design value of these rarely found pieces. Top: 2" bracelet of multicolored stones in elaborate filigree links, $200-300; below: a 4" heavy, goldplated fur clip with ruby red accents and elaborate crown, in a powerful figural design, $350-500.

These simple Freirich brooches are strikingly fashionable when grouped to march the length of a jacket lapel, $15-35 ea.

Calvaire

Information on Calvaire is sketchy. However, it appears to be the product of a French designer. The pieces are replete with meticulous detail, including brilliant stones, ormolu, wiring of beads, and delicate enameling. This jewelry most likely dates from the 1950s and 1960s and is extremely rare - a "find" for the collector! (see page 204 for example)

De Rosa

Founded in 1935 in New York as the Ralph DeRosa Company, it remained a family operation until production stopped in 1955. As was often the case during that era, some DeRosa pieces were paper-tagged or unmarked. Nevertheless, this high quality line can often be identified by their distinctive and beautiful designs. Their floral pieces are especially noteworthy, featuring rich enameling and unusual shadings, often tinged with reds and browns. Other offerings were equally breathtaking for their brilliant stones and masterful figural designs.

When one observes the similarity in quality, materials, and innovations, it's not surprising that for many years DeRosa operated in conjunction with Schiaparelli jewelry. Both were high-fashion lines with distinctive design qualities -- and both are highly desirable today.

Two exapmles of the versatility and beauty of DeRosa designs. The swan, with enormous blue center and sparkling rhinestone accents, has amber stones that create a graceful, fanlike effect, $800+. The elaborate enameled flower with aquamarine center stone carries the art of enameling to new heights, $300+. Both are clear evidence of why the DeRosa name is representative of the very finest in jewelry from the past.

From "Masterpieces of Costume Jewelry" by Ball and Torem. Photographs by Dorothy Torem.

Eclectic enameled alligator bracelet, $150-200, by Pauline Rader shares equal space with a Les Bernard red snake bracelet, $175-225; below is Karu brooch and earrings of enameled flowers interspersed with colored stones, $100-125; A Razza bull necklace, looking understandably perplexed, is in forefront, $85-135.

Two examples of the type of brooch that made Van S Authentics so popular with the younger, "hip" audience of the 1960s. Top, $125-175. Bottom, $125-150.

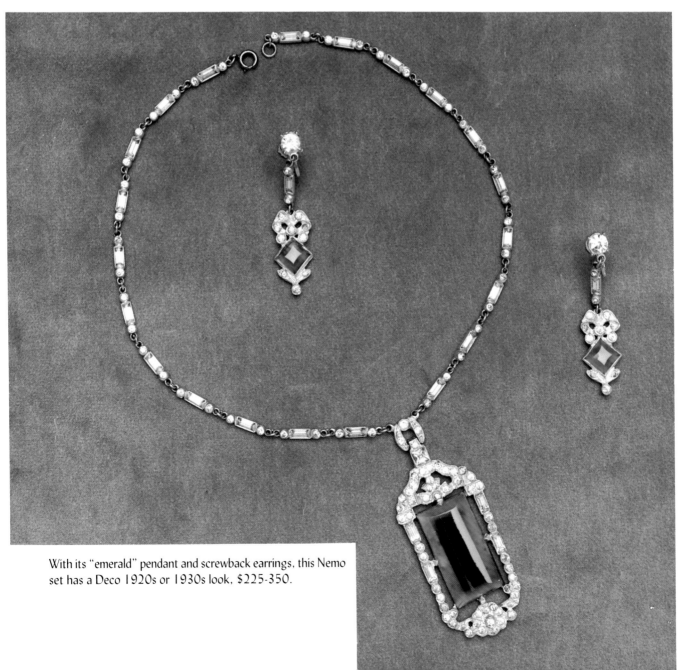

With its "emerald" pendant and screwback earrings, this Nemo set has a Deco 1920s or 1930s look, $225-350.

2" angel marked Mylu is captivating in its stylish grace, $50-65. Three dimensional 2½" brooch marked Ora is intriguing, with minarets, sparkling stones, and a center horn, $200-250.

This hippo with trembler head and red eye is a big game hunter's delight. Marked *Frank Buck, Bring 'Em Back Alive*, it's a rare and nostalgic capture! $375-450.

Three glistening bracelets by Matisse-Renoir effectively show why copper jewelry is enjoying such renewed interest. Left to right: $85-125; $65-85; $65-85.

Other Names to Look for

CRAFTSMAN/GEMCRAFT (founded by Alfeo Verrechia)
LEO GLASS (in operation from 1943-1957)
GEORGE JENSEN (sterling)
STANLEY HAGLER (Jewelry in the Haskell genre)
MATISSE/RENOIR (copper)
ORA (founded by Oreste Agnini in 1921)
CIRO (in operation since 1917, early pieces are a "find.")
VAN S. AUTHENTICS
WIESNER
HAR
MYLU
BRANIA
LAGUNA
REINAD
BARCLAY
SELRO
DeLILLO
MIMI DiN

These HAR pieces are charming examples of the captivating figurals that make HAR jewelry so distinctive and such great finds for the collector. $225-350 each.

And don't overlook some of the pieces made by:
BEAU (sterling) and Beau Jewels
BOGOFF
DANECRAFT (sterling)
NEMO
SERBIN
REGENCY
LISNER

GOLDETTE (trademark name of Circle Jewelry, owned by Ben Gartner and son Michael)
BSK (owned by Bernie Steinberg and Hy Slovitt)
RAZZA
KARU
NEMO
KORDA

The list could, of course, go on and on. Above all, let your own personal taste dictate your choices. Whether marked or unmarked, by famous designer or little-known artisan, expensive or a tag sale special, when a piece makes its way to your jewelry box and then onto a special (or not so special) outfit, you'll experience the unique thrill of discovering - and most especially *enjoying* - a treasure!

This masterful 2¾" Calvaire brooch (in forefront) has everything—a double layer of intricate filigree, with strands of woven gold creating a foundation for delicately enameled flowers, tiny pearls and cabochons, capped by huge, faceted stones in faux pink tourmaline, $650-850. The unsigned 5¾" Art Nouveau figure can be worn as a most compelling brooch, $125-200.

Bibliography

Baillen, Claude, *Chanel Solitaire*. Translated by Barbara Bray, New York: Quadrangle, 1974.

Baker, Lillian, *Fifty Years of Collectible Fashion Jewelry*, Paducah, Kentucky: Collectors Books, 1986.

Ball, Joanne Dubbs and Torem, Dorothy Hehl, "The Art of Fashion Accessories," Schiffer Publishing Ltd., Atglen, Pa., 1993.

Ball, Joanne Dubbs and Torem, Dorothy Hehl, "Masterpieces of Costume Jewelry," Schiffer Publishing Ltd., Atglen, Pa., 1993.

Berenson, Marissa, *Dressing Up*, New York: G.P. Putnam's Sons, 1984.

Carter, Ernestine, *Magic Names in Fashion*, Englewood Cliffs, New Jersey: Prentice-Hall, 1980.

Charles-Roux, Edmund, *Chanel*, New York: Alfred A. Knopf, 1975.

Cocteau, Jean, "Mademoiselle Chanel", *Harper's Bazaar*, New York: Hearst Corporation, 1954.

Dolan, Maryanne, *Collecting Rhinestone Colored Jewelry*, Florence, Alabama: Books Americana, 1989.

Fried, Eunice, "Faux but...Fabulous", *Almanac*. Franklin Center, Pennsylvania: Franklin Mint, November/December 1988.

Joseff, Eugene, "Let's Be Glamorous", *Movie Show*, New York: Liberty Magazine, Inc., 1948.

Klein, Mim, "A Look at Three Great Costume Jewelry Houses: Monet, Trifari, Haskell", *Collectors Clocks and Jewelry*, Holiday p. 68. West Chester, Pennsylvania: Schiffer Publishing, Ltd., 1988.

Madsen, Alex, *Living for Design - The Yves Saint Laurent Story*, New York: Delacorte Press, 1979.

McDowell, Colin, *McDowell's Directory of 20th Century Fashion*, Englewood Cliffs, New Jersey: Prentice-Hall, 1985.

Photoplay, February 1943.

Schiaparelli, *Shocking Life*, New York: E.P. Dutton and Co., Inc., 1954.

Stegmeyer, Ann, *Who' Who in Fashion*, New York: Fairchild Press, 1988.

Talley, André L., "Fanfair, A Taste for Paste," *Vanity Fair*, New York, Conde Nast Publications, Inc., October, 1987.

White, Palmer, *Elsa Schiaparelli: Empress of Paris Fashion*, New York: Rizzoli, 1986.